EXTREME METAL DRUMMING

By Hannes Grossmann

Edited by Rick Mattingly

Cover photo courtesy of Steven Chew for stevenchew.net

ISBN 978-1-4768-1421-6

HAL•LEONARD®
CORPORATION

7777 W. BLUEMOUND RD. P.O. BOX 13819 MILWAUKEE, WI 53213

In Australia Contact:
Hal Leonard Australia Pty. Ltd.
4 Lentara Court
Cheltenham, Victoria, 3192 Australia
Email: ausadmin@halleonard.com.au

Visit Hal Leonard Online at
www.halleonard.com

NOTATION LEGEND

Kick   Snare   Rack Tom 1   Rack Tom 2   Floor Tom   Hi-Hat   Ride   Ride Bell   Hi-Hat Open   Mini Tom   Crash   Splash   China   Choked Crash

CONTENTS

FOREWORD

by george kollias

Extreme metal drumming is a very special genre. It requires skill, technique, dedication, and hours and hours of practice, but also a lot of heart and soul. I know that very well. Some drummers outside extreme metal can only get some of what we do—speed would be a perfect example. But to me, there is a lot more: I need to feel the groove!

Many drummers wonder if it's even possible to groove at those extreme tempos, but it is, and that's what, in my opinion, separates the good musician from the average one. Even if a drummer has the technique to go super fast, I still wonder, "Can he make music? Can he make people move?"

There are drummers in this genre who are very special to me because they combine all the elements I need from a musician. They can play super fast, but also very musically. They can navigate a 13/8 groove so smoothly, it leaves other drummers clueless about time and meter. They can throw a fill in the midst of a blast beat that makes me go, "What was that?" Hannes Grossmann is one of these few drummers. Hannes combines all the elements a GREAT drummer should have onstage and offstage. I will never forget watching him for the first time on a tour in Japan, and I thought, "Man, this guy sounds even better than on the album!" I'm very proud to know him, and very motivated by his drumming. Period!

George Kollias

ACKNOWLEDGMENTS

Thanks to Tina for love and support; also thanks to my parents, Rainer and Renate Grossmann; my bandmates in Obscura and Blotted Science; the people and bands I've worked and played with so far; everyone at Meinl Cymbals, especially Marcus Lipperer, Stephan Haenisch, and Norbert Saemann; all the people at Tama Drums, especially Rocky Oda and Mick Suyama; everyone at Hal Leonard Corporation; Matthias Landes; V.Santura; and George Kollias.

   A special thanks goes to Alex Webster for introducing me to the people at Hal Leonard and opening this door. Your book *Extreme Metal Bass* builds the foundation for the release of *Extreme Metal Drumming* and has greatly helped to motivate and inspire me to write this book.

   Hannes Grossmann plays Meinl cymbals, Tama drums, Vic Firth sticks, and Evans drumheads exclusively.

INTRODUCTION

For a long time, extreme metal was a playing style unknown to a major part of the drumming community. During the last ten years, extreme metal drumming established a great reputation in the drum world, and today many musicians at least have an idea of how modern metal drumming sounds. In fact, it drastically differs from the bad image metal drumming had among most drummers in the past. Extreme metal drumming evolved from hard rock and heavy metal of the 1970s and '80s, but in its actual form it has little to do with its origin. Not even considering that the term extreme metal is an umbrella term that includes many sub-genres— death metal, black metal, thrash metal, deathcore, doom, grind, and sludge (among others)—modern metal drumming generally features a vast amount of technicality, fast and complex double-bass patterns, odd time signatures, erratic song structures, and in many cases, a tempo that goes beyond 200 beats per minute. Hence a modern extreme metal drummer has to acquire diverse skills to be able to play the music. You could argue that speed and technicality don't have their own musical value, which is true. But by interacting with other instruments and considering song arrangements, dynamics, timing, and a great feel, you can use the technicality and the high tempo to express yourself musically and create something unique.

So you got your copy of *Extreme Metal Drums*—thank you very much, by the way—for a good reason: to learn the most common techniques and their applications used in extreme metal drumming. Therefore, in the first part of the book you'll learn the best warm-up methods (chapter 1) and ways to build up and improve your double-bass technique (chapter 2); you'll find out about a special concept of extreme metal drumming—the blast beat—and how to play and practice various types of blast beats (chapter 3). You'll learn ways to build up and improve speed and endurance most effectively (chapter 4), and, of course, you'll find many exercises about how to phrase fills (chapter 5).

In the second part of the book you'll get to know how groove playing can be adapted to extreme metal (chapter 6) and how blast beats can be used in a musical context (chapter 7). Therefore you'll find many examples of how to accompany guitar riffs and how to phrase various patterns musically. The book features more advanced ways of double-bass playing (chapter 8), but it also shows how to overcome technical limitations that haven't been negotiated yet (chapter 9). In the end, you'll find three song examples featuring all the techniques and phrasings you've learned.

So have fun with the examples and exercises presented in this book. Besides helping you to improve your drumming skills, I hope it will also inspire you to write and perform your own music.

 TRACK 1

HOW TO USE THIS BOOK

This book is mainly written for intermediate and advanced players, which means you should know the most common basics already. I'd recommend having played the drums for at least one year. *Extreme Metal Drums* features two main parts: fundamentals and musical application. Depending on your level of playing, you need to practice intensely the chapters in part 1 before moving on to part 2. Chapters 1, 2, 3, and 4 build the basis for the following chapters. I recommend going through these chapters chronologically first. You can build your own practice schedule by mixing different exercises of the first four chapters, since they interlock with each other. Chapter 5 features all sorts of fills. You'll need these exercises to play through many examples of part 2, but chapter 5 also works independently from the second part of the book. Chapters 2, 3, and 4 are the foundation for chapters 6 and 7. So make sure to understand fully the first part of the book before seriously working on part 2. Chapter 8 is a special extension of chapter 2, so be careful: It might be too difficult if you haven't mastered the earlier chapters yet. Chapter 9 is more practical and already shows ways to deal with difficult situations in a band context. Before playing the songs in chapter 10, all previous chapters need to be fully mastered.

If not indicated otherwise, all exercises and examples in this book are in 4/4. The tempo is up to your individual level of playing. Practice all exercises without a metronome first, but also try to work with a click track once an exercise feels comfortable to you. Also work with the CD and listen closely to the audio examples. This book is written by a right-handed player, so all exercises need to be understood this way. If you're left-handed, feel free to invert the sticking.

ABOUT THE CD

The included CD features audio tracks of examples and exercises shown in the book. Some of them are play-along tracks with guitar, bass, and click track, or feature a full-band play-along. Every example in the book appearing on the CD is marked by this audio sign: 🔊

CD CREDITS

All material written, recorded, and produced by Hannes Grossmann
Drums and guitar recorded by Hannes Grossmann at the Hemisphere Studios
Bass programming by Hannes Grossmann

CD TRACK LIST

PART I
FUNDAMENTALS

CHAPTER 1
WARMING UP

Extreme metal is a very physically demanding style of music. Often you'll have to execute a lot of fast notes over many measures, hit hard, and challenge the volume of the screaming, heavily distorted guitars. Playing powerfully is important to provide the listener with the distinct "aggressive" or heavy feel the music needs. Taking this into account, I would like to start the book with introducing helpful warm-up exercises in order to prevent injuries due to hard and frequent hitting.

In this style of music it is best to use single strokes for warming up. Single strokes are the most basic rudiment, and to play singles, you don't need to be a technically profound player or to develop special technical skills. They work equally well for beginners and intermediate players, but also for professional drummers. I collected the following exercises over the years, and I can guarantee that they'll work. Most of these exercises can be played on a practice pad as well.

THE "GROWING STROKES" METHOD

This exercise is a great starting point for warming up. The basic method was inspired by Simon Phillips, but I created my own version of it, which works even more effectively for extreme metal drumming (see exercise 1-1a):

- Set up a quarter-note click track that you follow with your left foot on the hi-hat.

- Start playing alternating singles strokes for two measures.

- Immediately switch to doubles and play those for two measures.

- Increase the interval of the strokes: play three strokes per hand, then four, five, six, seven, and eight. Each interval must be repeated at least four times!

When playing three, five, and seven strokes per hand, you go through several odd-time signatures, which might confuse you at first. But it just takes a couple of attempts to play the exercise fluently. The tempo is not very important here. Choose a slower tempo and execute all strokes accurately rather than rushing through the exercise.

Exercise 1-1a

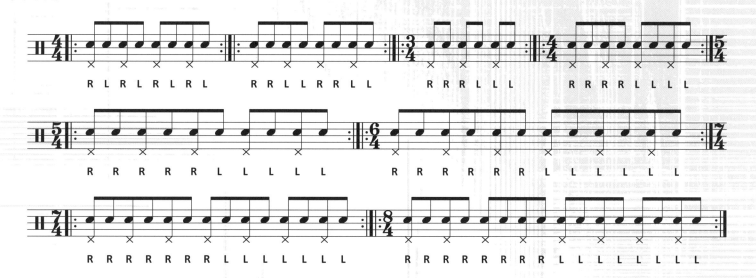

You can apply this exercise to your feet as well:

Exercise 1-1b

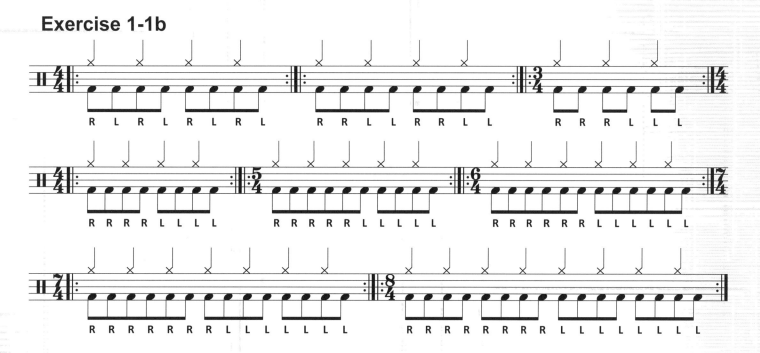

WARMING UP FINGERS

If you're one of those drummers who use their fingers quite a lot (like me), it makes sense to warm them up as well. The same method works for generally improving your finger-control technique:

- Get your hand into a French grip (which means the thumb is on top), and hold the stick with the thumb and index finger only.
- Play 8 measures in a comfortable tempo by only using the middle finger.
- Play 8 measures in a comfortable tempo by only using the ring finger.
- Play 8 measures in a comfortable tempo by only using the little finger.
- Once you have trained each finger individually, play single strokes for 24 measures using all the fingers together.

Exercise 1-2

THE "CHESS FIELD" METHOD

Just as you increased the number of single strokes in exercise 1-1, you can now raise the number of whole measures step by step. Set the metronome at a comfortable tempo and play single strokes with the right hand for one measure, then immediately switch to the left hand and play one measure (see exercise 1-3a). Then switch back and play two measures with the right hand, then two measures with the left hand. From now on, double the number of measures played by each hand: execute 4 measures, then 8, then 16, 32, and finally 64 (each hand separately). Make sure to start at a tempo you'll be able to maintain during this long-distance single-stroke exercise.

Exercise 1-3a

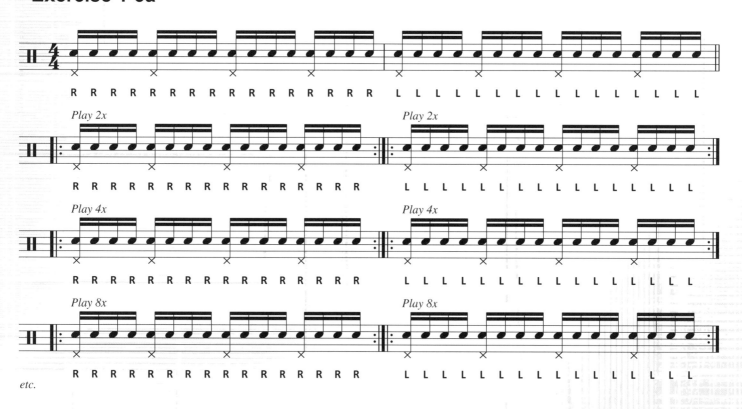

This method also works for your feet (see exercise 1-3b). You just need to play a regular 4/4 backbeat and have the right foot play single strokes for one measure, then switch to the left foot. Then increase the number of measures as explained above.

Exercise 1-3b

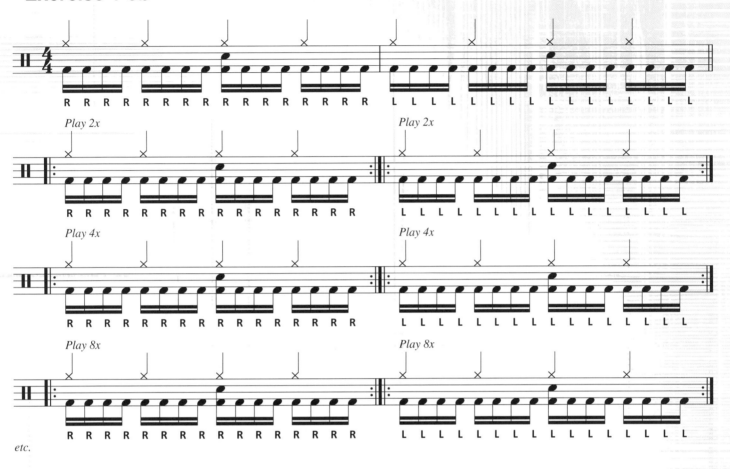

Play 2x   *Play 2x*

Play 4x   *Play 4x*

Play 8x   *Play 8x*

etc.

You can even extend the exercise and make a game out of it. There are two possible setups:

1. Measure Setup: Set the tempo pretty slow, and try to play as many measures as possible by doubling the number each time (32, 64, 128, 256...).

2. Tempo Setup: Set the number of measures played to fixed number, for instance 32. Start at a moderate tempo and play through the 32 measures. Then progressively increase the tempo by 5 bpm. The goal is to play the same number of measures as fast as possible.

Note: I call this method the "Chess Field Method," referring to the so-called "exponential equation"—a mathematical function that describes how numbers increase when you continually double them. So if you put one dollar on the first field of a chess game, then two dollars on the second, four dollars on the third, and so on, how many dollars do you get in the end? It's a total of 18,446,744,073,709,551,615 dollars! So be careful when you double the amount of measure; it easily might get out of hand! Rather, include steps in between, like 24 or 42 measures.

PRECISION

In the same way you need the ability to hear fast when you want to play fast, you need to be able to hear timing accurately to really develop a good time feel. Exercise 1-4 is a useful, basic exercise that reminds your ear of the accurate time feel. It contains a 2-over-3 pattern, with your right hand playing quarter notes and your left hand (and later your right foot) playing overlapping dotted-eighth notes. When repeating the pattern, the order of hands change: in the second bar your left hand plays quarters and your right hand dotted-eighth notes.

Exercise 1-4

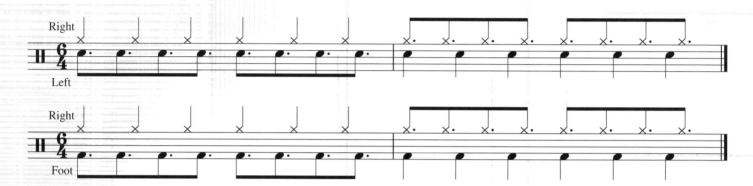

Now the most important thing: set up a sixteenth-note click track at a low tempo, like 70 or 80 bpm, and try to hit every note spot-on. Play at different volume levels as well. Then switch back to a quarter-note click and try to feel every sixteenth-note subdivision. Finally, set the click to a large interval, like whole measures, and play the exercise. By changing the click track's basic pulse, you can prove if your internal time feel is able to adapt to accurate subdivisions. This also works for other rhythms; I just find the 2-over-3 phrasing to be the most helpful for controlling precision on the drumkit.

WARMING UP WITHOUT DRUMS

Sometimes I forget to bring my practice pad and don't find out until half an hour before the show starts. So what to do then? Don't worry; there are still some basic exercises you can do to warm up your body without sitting behind the kit (or practice pad).

For warming up your hands, just simulate the wrist motion. Open your hands and "play" alternating single strokes at a comfortable tempo. This just means to move your hands up and down in the air. Try to do that with both hands for five minutes without taking a break. Maybe it is better not to "perform" this exercise in front of other people, since playing on imaginary drums definitely creates some scornful looks, especially from guitarists.

You can apply the same method to your feet. Just lift up the heel and let it fall onto the ground. Repeat that motion constantly at a comfortable tempo.

It can also be very helpful to jump up and down a little or do a few pushups. To me, it is important to get muscles warmed up and the bloodstream at "playing temperature," especially before a live show. It is also helpful to listen to music that inspires you and makes you want to play the drums. Seeking motivation to play might be the best warm-up. There are also a lot of mental workouts, but it is beyond the scope of this book to discuss those. I find it very helpful to go through song structures and sing guitar riffs and melodies in my head, silently. Whatever works for you is right. But don't think that coffee or energy drinks really help you to play better. They are placebos!

Note: Warming Up with Rudiments
*Double strokes, flam exercises, paradiddles, and other combinations also warm up the muscles, but differently and not as effectively as single strokes. In extreme metal, single strokes are more in the focus of playing than in most other genres. For instance, if you warm up with stick control combinations for half an hour and then try to play a blast beat, it probably won't work as well as if you'd warmed up with single strokes. However, making **additional** warm-ups include doubles, paradiddles, or any other rudiments is a good thing to do.*

CHAPTER 2
DOUBLE-BASS TECHNIQUES

Double-bass drumming is, without a doubt, one of the most frequently used concepts in extreme metal music. Therefore, being able to play double-bass patterns diversely and to fully control both feet are the most crucial things an extreme metal drummer has to master. In this chapter I've put together the most common ways of approaching double-bass playing. Furthermore, you'll find exercises on how to develop your double kick flexibility most effectively.

For all the exercises of this chapter, be careful with the tempo! You'll have to find the right tempo to start with, and then slightly increase it. Start practicing these exercises without a metronome/click track, and do not use a metronome before at least two weeks of steady practicing.

BASIC HAND-FOOT PATTERNS

The best way to get started with double-bass drumming, but also to improve and constantly train intermediate and advanced skills, is by playing steady alternating single strokes at various tempos, combined with specific hand patterns. Each of the basic patterns below creates its own musical feeling. The upbeat pattern (basic pattern 1) feels more forward driven, the downbeat pattern (2) more straight, and the backbeat pattern (3) has a somewhat "heavier" vibe to it. Depending on the individual musical situation, you'll have to find out which type fits best.

TRACK 2

Example 2-1

Basic Pattern 1: Upbeat

Basic Pattern 2: Downbeat

Basic Pattern 3: Backbeat

MIXING SIXTEENTH, THIRTY-SECOND AND TRIPLET NOTE VALUES

The exercises below feature one-bar-phrases based on sixteenth notes that are interspersed by various groups of sixteenth-note triplets and thirty-second notes. With each exercise these groups constantly shift, which will enable you to drastically improve your flexibility and short-term speed. The hands are written as backbeat patterns, but of course it's also possible to vary the hand pattern in the way shown in the section above (Basic Hand-Foot Patterns) or even come up with new ones. Here's an example of how to vary the hands:

Example 2-2

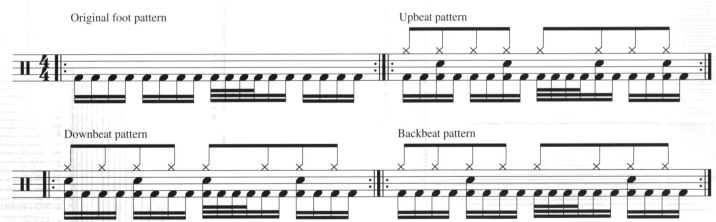

Original foot pattern

Upbeat pattern

Downbeat pattern

Backbeat pattern

Exercises

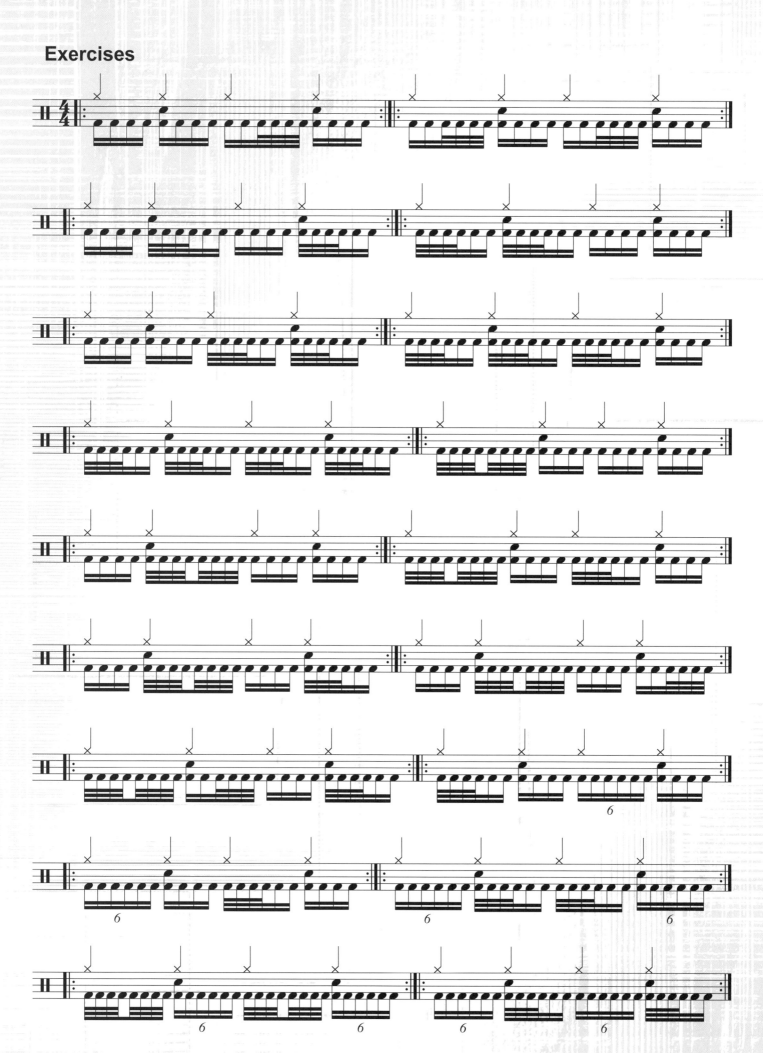

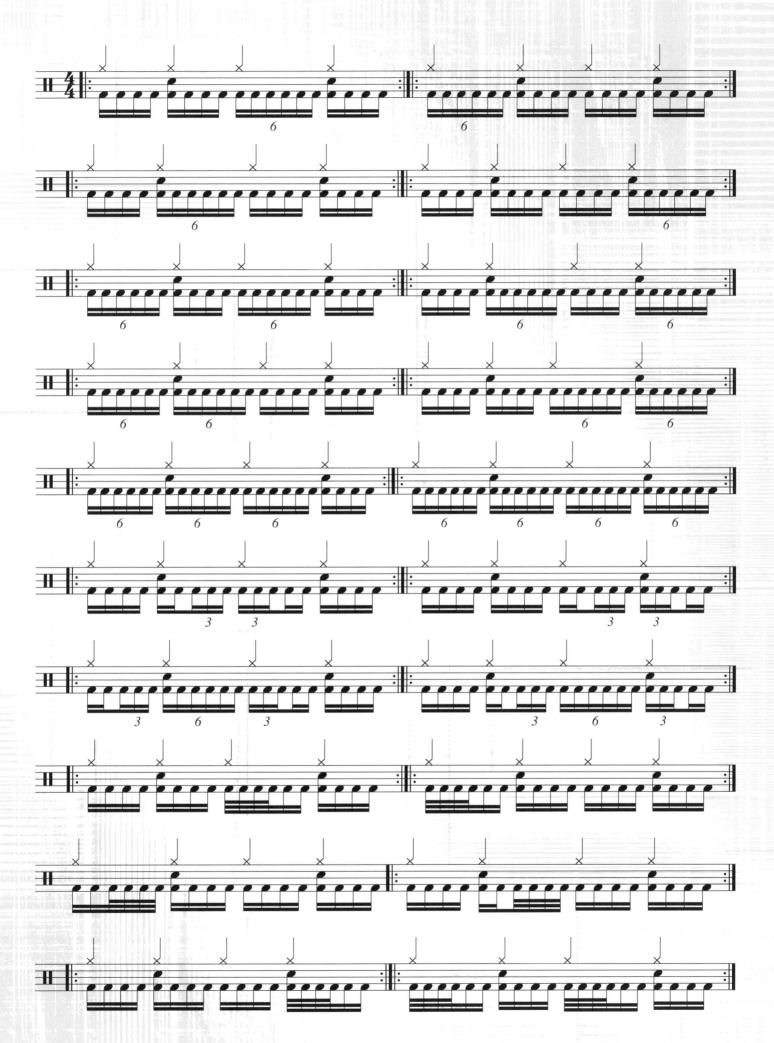

BREAKDOWN PATTERNS

Besides using ongoing alternating double kick patterns, it is very common in extreme metal to accent the kick drums together with the rhythm guitar, thus creating unison patterns based on various groups of eighth and sixteenth notes. These groups have a certain number of sequential notes—mostly three, five, and eight. This kind of playing is often used in subgenres like metal core, death core, and modern thrash metal. Typically, in the middle of a faster song, the tempo slows down and the whole band plays these sequential unison rhythms in order to create a musical "breakdown." On the enclosed CD, the following example, which shows basic breakdown patterns, is played at two different tempos: 100 and 150 bpm.

🔊 TRACK 3

Example 2-3

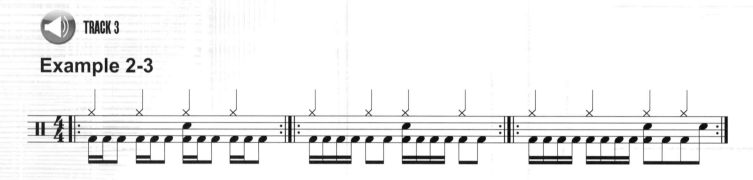

Below you'll find exercises on how to phrase breakdown patterns in various ways. Of course, there are many more options for phrasing a pattern, but these exercises at least give you a good starting point. Sometimes the snare drum is syncopated, which makes the patterns sound more interesting, but also more challenging. Example 2-4 illustrates the difference between an "even" hand phrasing and a more syncopated one. Depending on the musical situation, you'll have to choose which one feels and fits better. After having explored these exercises and developed a certain vocabulary regarding double-kick phrasings, be creative and make up your own patterns.

Example 2-4

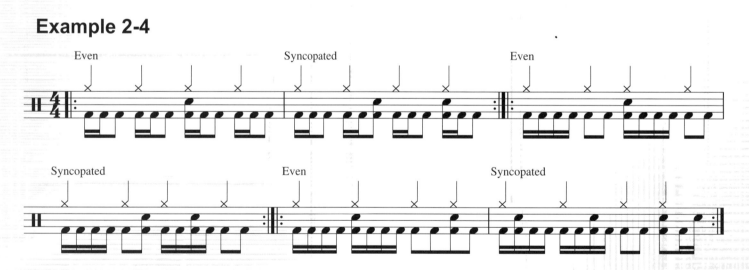

Breakdown Exercises

$\quad$ = 100–200

SYNCHRONIZING HAND-AND-FOOT SYNCOPATION

If you want to accent other counts than just the upbeat or downbeat, you'll have to further synchronize your hands with your feet. I've set up various exercises on how to play different kinds of accents with hands while using constantly alternating double-bass patterns. But be careful! Double-kick drumming becomes very difficult whenever a right-hand accent is crossed by a left foot, and vice versa. It's not always avoidable, so you need to learn how to do it. In the Synchronization Exercises 1 on the next page, the left hand is always on the snare, the right hand always on the hi-hat.

It is important to always sync your hands and feet, not just when playing even single strokes. Part 2 of the synchronization exercises feature ongoing sixteenth-note patterns that are interspersed by various groups of thirty-second notes. With every sixteenth-note group, you'll have to play hands in sync with feet, which means on every right foot there's a right hand on the ride cymbal, and every left foot is backed by a left hand on the hi-hat. Whenever a thirty-second-note pattern comes up, you can play it with the **hands alternating (R–L–R–L)**, or you can change the hand pattern to **double strokes (R–R–L–L)** (see example 2-5).

 TRACK 4

Example 2-5

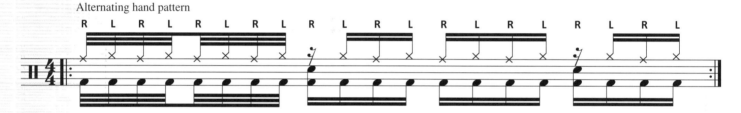

Synchronization Exercises 1

Synchronization Exercises 2

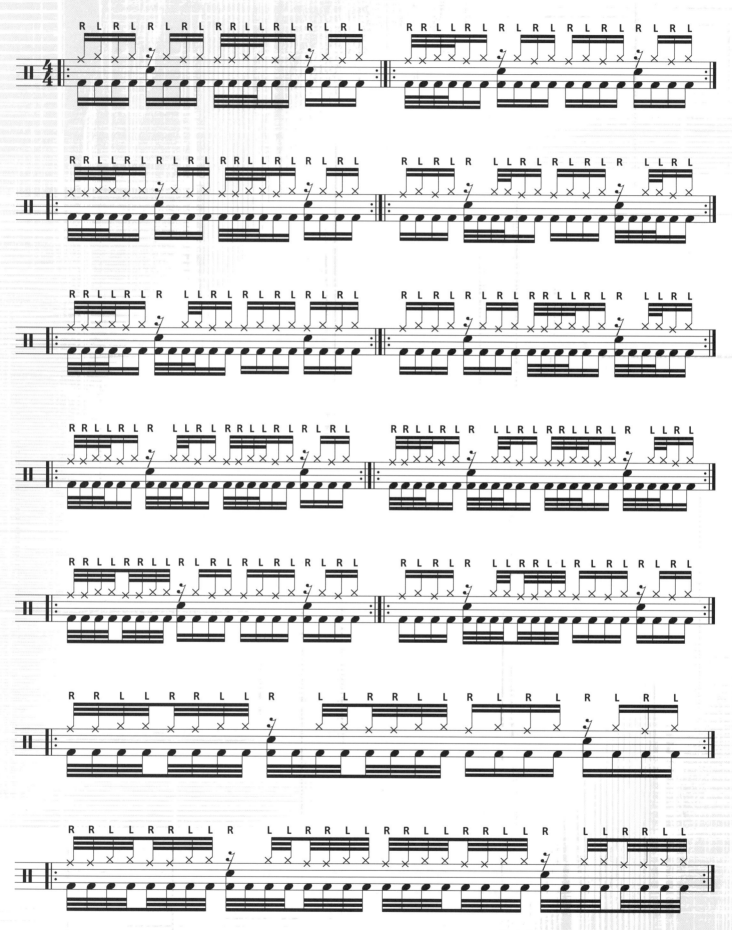

CHAPTER 3
BLAST BEAT TECHNIQUES

Nowadays, the blast beat is not only utilized in many different styles of extreme metal, but it has even become one of the main beat concepts within the genre. In the early days of extreme metal, the blast beat was used more as an effect for the sake of noise and delivering frantic energy to the audience, rather than being a real musical groove concept. By being played precisely and defining a time signature, the blast beat could be used as some sort of pulse, comparable to the swing feel in jazz music. Musically, the blast beat can have different roles, depending on when and how it is played (more specific information on the musical interpretation of blast beats can be found in chapter 7). In this chapter you'll learn about the different types of blasts and also find useful exercises to develop the most common accents and phrasings.

INTRODUCING DIFFERENT BLAST BEAT TYPES

In general, the blast beat can be described as a repeated sixteenth-note figure of fast, alternating single strokes between the bass drum and the left hand on the snare, while the right hand is playing lead accents on the ride, crash, or hi-hat cymbal. Example 3-1a illustrates the basic blast beat pattern, the so-called "traditional blast" (or alternating blast). As you can see, kick and right hand on the hi-hat play in unison on even and off-beat counts (1, 1-and, 2, 2-and, etc.), and the left hand plays the sixteenth-note subdivisions in between the kicks (1-e, 1-a, 2-e, 2-a, etc.).

 TRACK 5

Example 3-1a: The Traditional Blast Beat

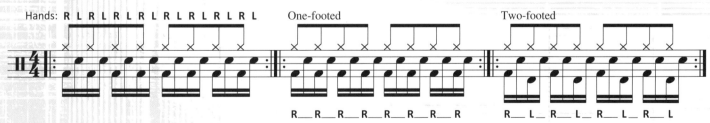

The notes on the bass drum can be executed by one foot only or both feet alternating. Both ways create their own playing feel, but musically it doesn't make a difference since the note value stays the same. The decision to play a blast beat with one foot or two feet is individual. There is no right or wrong way. For both methods you can find examples of well-known extreme metal drummers: Pete Sandoval, Derek Roddy, and George Kollias play the blast one-footed, while Dave Culross, Dirk Verbeuren, and Gene Hoglan play it with both feet.

In metal music, the blast originally emerged from the so-called skank beat, which was previously used in thrash metal (with bands like Slayer, Kreator, or early Metallica). So you can understand the blast beat as a double-time skank beat (see example 3-1b). Pete Sandoval was one of the first drummers to use this switching from skank to blast beat on Morbid Angel's famous debut album, *Altars of Madness*, and Terrorizer's *World Downfall*, both released in 1989.

 TRACK 6

Example 3-1b: Skank Beat vs. Blast Beat

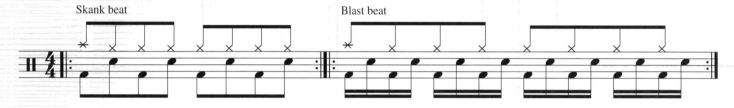

A blast is often played as triplets:

 TRACK 7

Exercise 3-1c: Triplet Blast

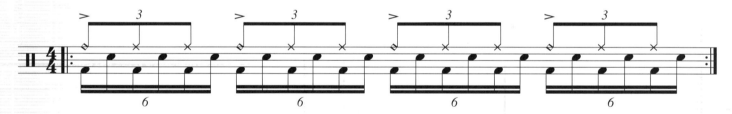

Just like the swing pulse in jazz, there are various concepts of how to play a blast beat. Example 3-2a illustrates a non-alternating blast or "hammer blast." Here you don't play alternating sixteenth-note single strokes, but eighth notes with the right hand, left hand, and feet in unison. This type of blast beat usually sounds more basic and provides the listener with a raw feel. Often this beat is used to express a certain brutality. A famous example of how to use this blast type musically is in the music of legendary New York death metal band Suffocation. Like in example 3-2b, snare fills are often thrown in the beat to accent a guitar riff.

Example 3-2a: Non-Alternating Blast Beat

Example 3-2b: Non-Alternating Blast with Snare Fills

The so-called "bomb blast" can be found in example 3-3a. The basis for this type of beat would be a non-alternating blast pattern, but now the kick drums play steady sixteenth notes. One of the first bands to use this kind of blast beat was Cannibal Corpse, one of extreme metal's most popular bands. Often the bomb blast is played as triplets (see example 3-3b).

Unlike the traditional blast beat, in a bomb blast the cymbal accents are played by the left hand, and the right hand plays on the snare. (Of course, you can do it the other way around as well.) Start practicing the following exercises slowly, and make sure that hands and feet are in sync.

Example 3-3a: Bomb Blast

Example 3-3b: Triplet Bomb Blast

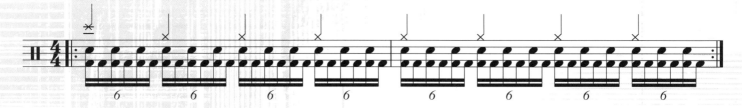

A more modern type of blast beat is the "gravity blast," which is technically very demanding. You play sixteenth notes on the kick drum and back those with a one-handed sixteenth-note roll on the snare drum (see example 3-4). The one-handed roll is executed by laying the stick on the drum and moving it up and down on the rim. For specific information about this technique, check out Johnny Rabb's videos. A very detailed description can be found on Jojo Mayer's *Secret Weapons* DVD.

In a gravity blast the eighth-note cymbal accents typically shift to quarter notes. Examples of bands that use this kind of blast are Origin (USA), Beneath the Massacre (Canada), and Defeated Sanity (Germany), among others.

Example 3-4: The Gravity Blast

The latest innovation among blast beats is backbeat blasts, which are basically traditional blasts with the right hand occasionally playing accents on the snare by moving from the ride/hi-hat to the snare. The left hand is executing singles as ghost notes on a second snare drum or a tom, since the main snare is occupied by the right hand doing accents. Examples 3-5a and 3-5b illustrate the most typical backbeat blast phrasings.

Example 3-5a: Backbeat Blast 1

TRACK 14

Example 3-5b: Backbeat Blast 2

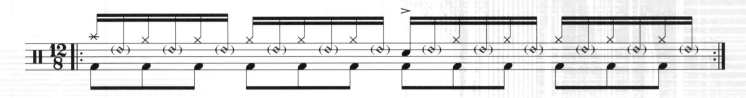

I first saw Derek Roddy doing this kind of backbeat blast. An adaption of this concept can be heard in the song "Osiris" by German black metal artists Dark Fortress.

Note: Educational Material
If you are interested in learning more about the blast beat, check out Derek Roddy's book The Evolution of Blast Beats. *For a more visual conception, I recommend George Kollias' DVDs* Intense Metal Drumming 1 and 2, *or my own DVD,* Progressive Concepts for the Modern Metal Drummer.

How to Learn and Practice Blast Beats

The definition of the (traditional) blast beat referring to alternating single strokes between feet and left hand might imply that you need to slow down and practice the foot/left-hand combination relentlessly without using the right hand. However, you don't necessarily need to do that. Looking at example 3-1a in a different way, you can see you're also playing alternating sixteenth-note single strokes with your hands.

Example 3-1a: Broken Down

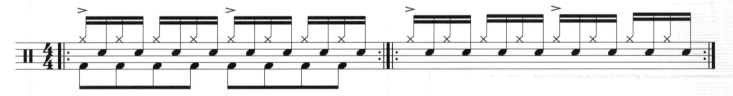

Hence, you could also interpret the blast beat as alternating single strokes made by hands, while every right hand is backed by a kick drum. All you need to do then is synchronize your right hand with your feet.

Example 3-6 shows exactly how to do that: Just play alternating sixteenth notes with your hands, accenting every quarter note with the right hand. Then integrate the right foot and play every quarter note along with the hands. Then play eighth notes with the feet while keeping the sixteenth-note roll on the snare. The last step to finally playing a blast beat is alternating the right hand between the snare and the ride cymbal.

TRACK 15

Exercise 3-6

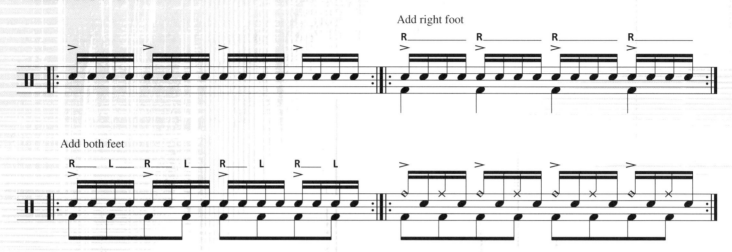

If you want to improve a specific blast beat phrasing, you also need to synchronize your right hand with the feet. Therefore, first execute your right hand on the cymbal in unison with your feet for at least 8 measures. Second, the left hand must not be neglected, so for getting your hands in balance, just play the same amount of measures with your left hand only. In a third step you integrate specific accents into a snare roll, and finally you apply them to a regular blast. You can practice all kinds of right-hand accents this way. Example 3-7 just shows one specific pattern. This way of practicing can be applied to all the combinations following in Chapter 3 B.

TRACK 16

Exercise 3-7

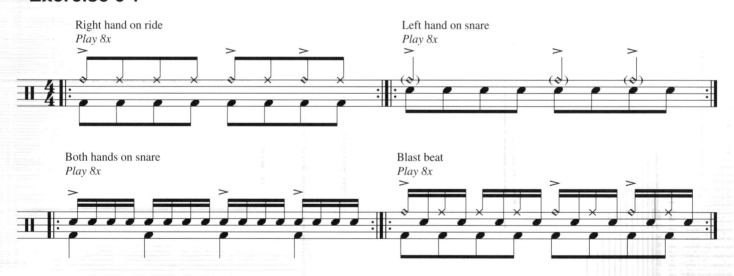

Note: Click Track

Once you feel comfortable with this technique, practice blast beats to a metronome. At such high tempos it is very important to develop good timing, because even a small inaccuracy can blur the conciseness a blast beat should have. I strongly recommend practicing with a quarter-note click track on half time. For instance, if you play sixteenth notes at 200 bpm, set the metronome to 100 and use a quarter-note click. This way, you'll get a better feel for all the fast sixteenth-note subdivisions.

BLAST SYNCOPATION AND ACCENTS

Now that I've introduced various types of blast beats, the next pages contain specific exercises on how to phrase blast beats. In these exercises your right hand is executing lead accents on the ride bell, placed on different counts. By practicing various accents on the ride bell, you'll improve your control and independence. Of course, you can apply those accents to all other types of blast beats as well. Also feel free to create your own melodies by playing the accents on various cymbals, not only on the ride bell.

Just like previously illustrated in example 3-7, I strongly recommend you synchronize the right hand and the feet before practicing a complete pattern. All these patterns can also be played as **non-alternating blast beats**.

Exercises: Traditional Blasts

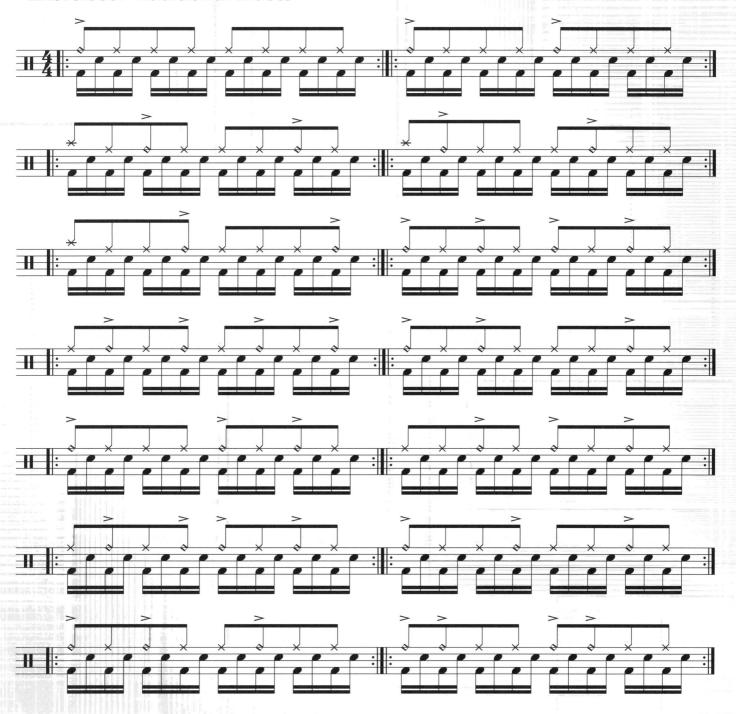

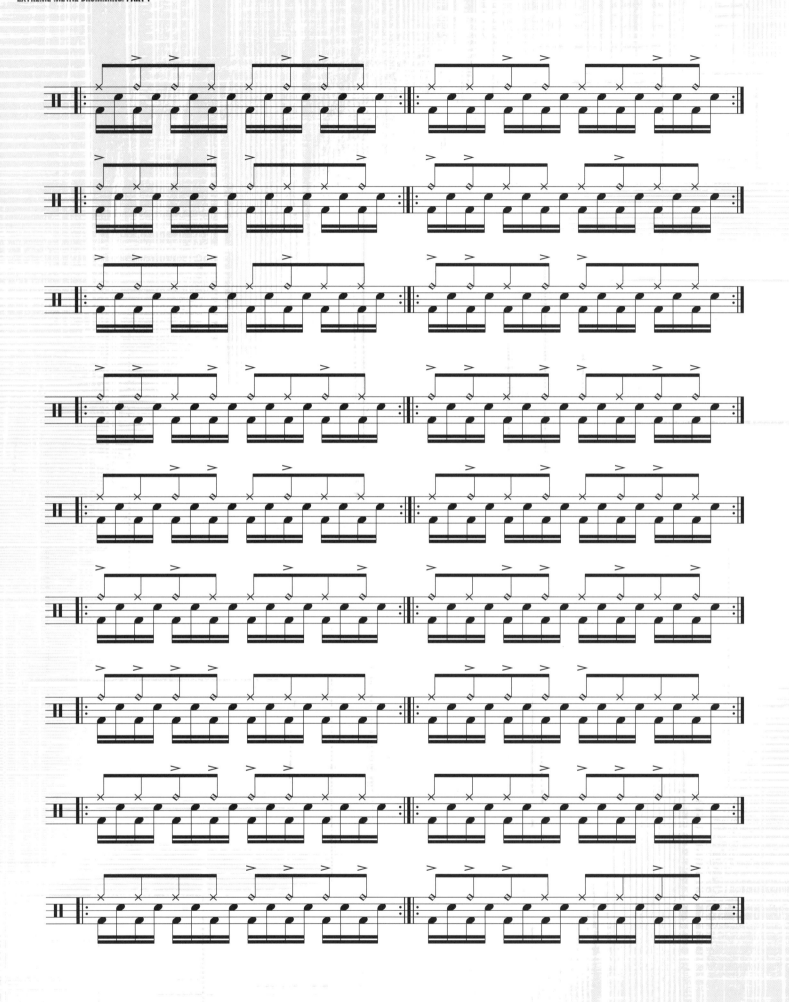

bomb blast syncopation

A very similar type of syncopation can also be applied to bomb blasts. In my opinion, not every traditional blast pattern sounds equally good when interpreted as a bomb blast, because a bomb blast contains twice as many notes played by the feet. This makes the sound a little fussy at times. But that's just a matter of personal taste. You might have noticed that in extreme metal, the "less-is-more" concept isn't valid anyway.

Exercises: Bomb Blasts

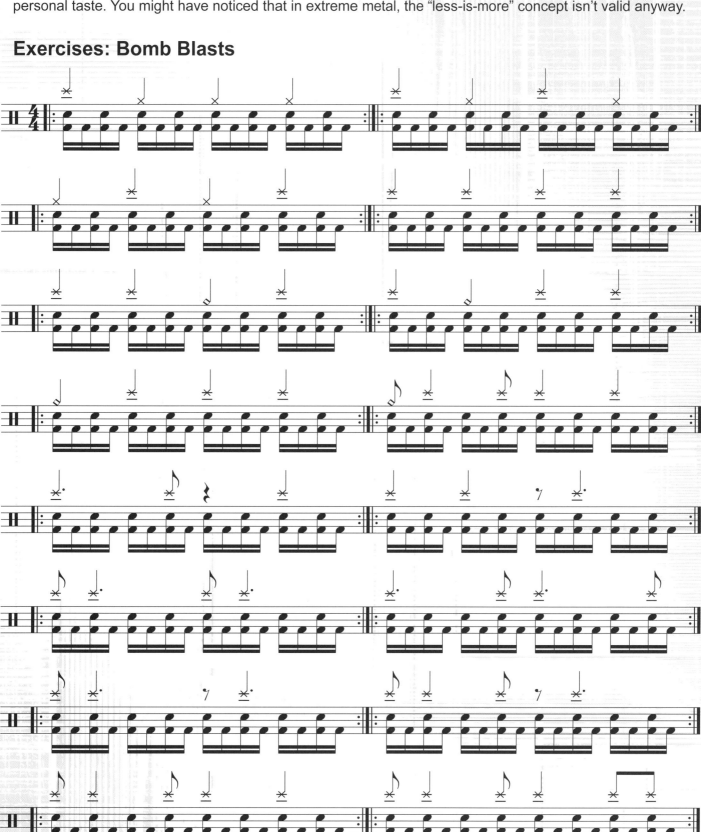

syncopation with choked cymbals

Stopping a cymbal on various accents is extremely common in the death metal genre. It is often used in fills and non-alternating blast beats.

 **TRACK 17**

Example 3-8a:

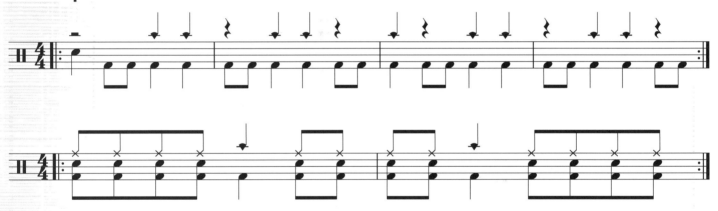

It is also possible to integrate faster sixteenth-note kick rolls before choking the cymbal.

 TRACK 18

Example 3-8b:

Here are some exercises that will help you to use cymbal chokes.

Exercises: Cymbal Chokes

triplet syncopation

Blast beats are often played as triplets. Here are some exercises showing the most common accents. But be careful! With the meter changing to triplets, the tempo has to change as well. Every pattern is played as a traditional blast, but if you want to create additional homework, you can also interpret every phrase as its bomb-blast twin.

Example 3-9

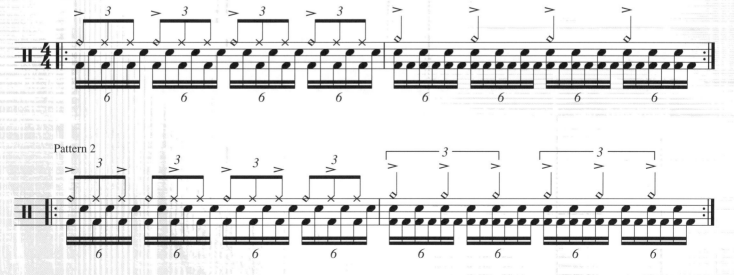

Exercises: Triplet Blasts

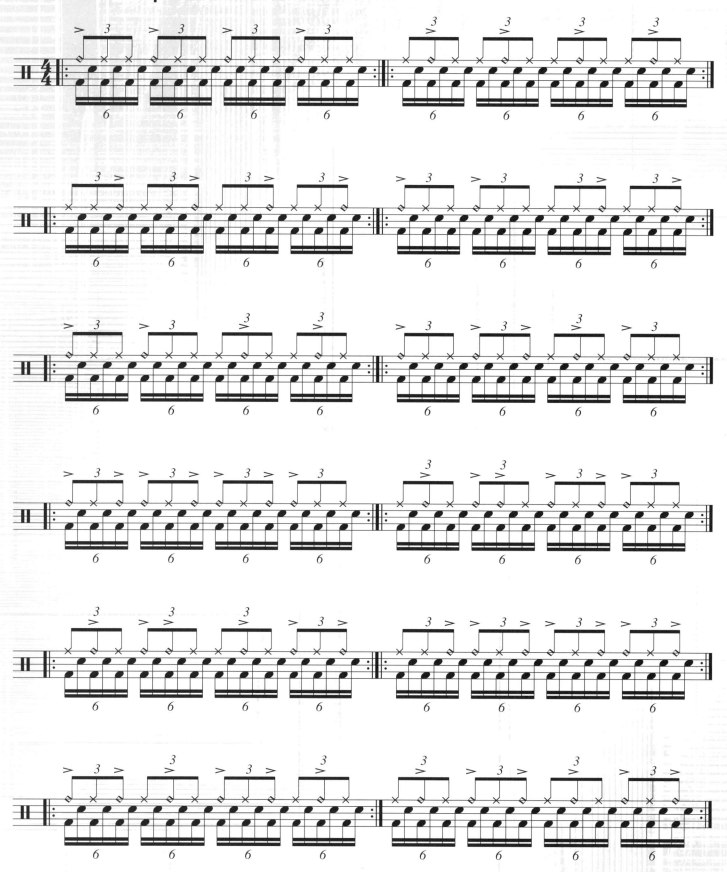

INTEGRATING FAST DOUBLE-BASS ROLLS INTO BLASTS

Since you've previously learned blast phrasings and double-bass exercises, you should now be able to put both concepts together. The following exercises integrate sixteenth-note kick rolls and fast triplets into various blast beat phrasings. Since we're dealing with two-bar phrases, make sure to practice slowly at first. Feel free to create your own patterns by mixing up these exercises.

Exercises: Integrating Fast Double-Bass Rolls

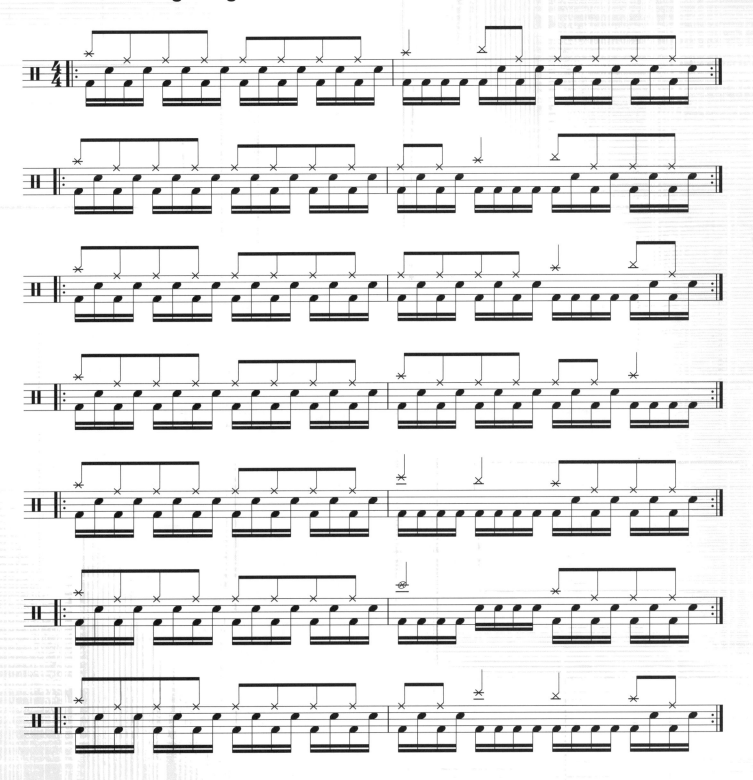

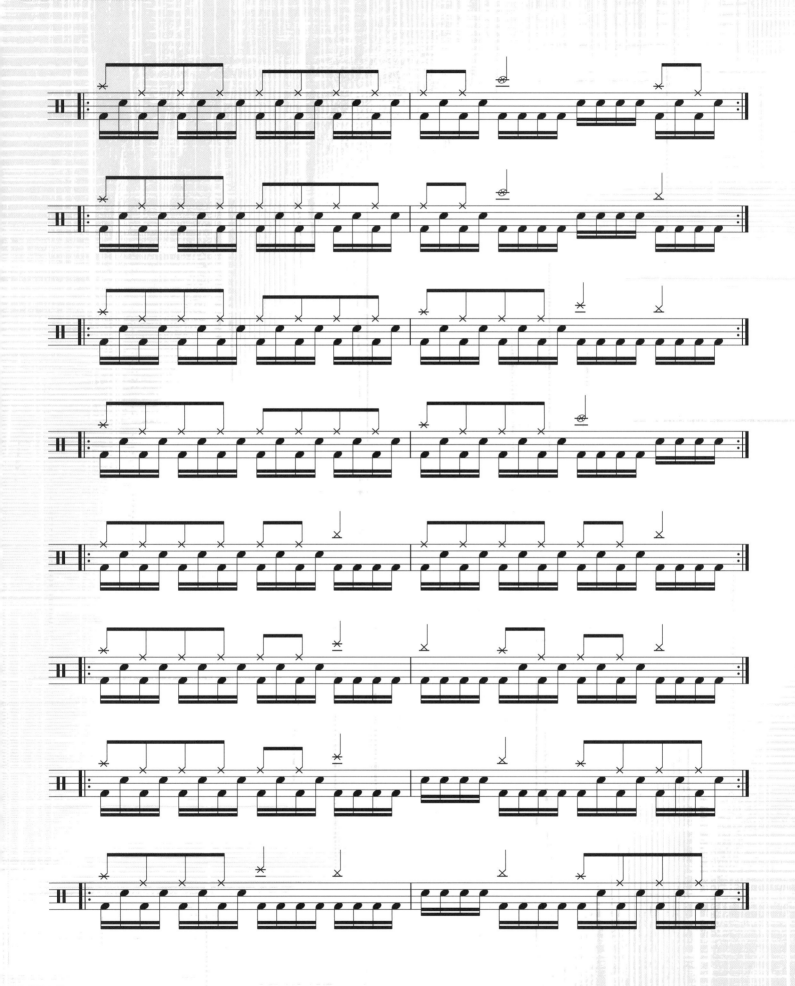

Exercises with Triplet Insertion

CHAPTER 4
IMPROVING SPEED AND ENDURANCE

From the early days on, the innovators of extreme metal have recognized the musical intensity of fast playing. In the mid/late 1980s, bands like Sodom, Kreator, Morbid Angel, Napalm Death, Terrorizer, Possessed, and, of course, Slayer, utilized speed as a key factor to make their music sound "extreme." Nowadays, since overall playing technique has further evolved, it's very common to play fast and maintain a high tempo throughout one or even several songs. Therefore a modern drummer who wants to master all relevant styles of extreme metal has to acquire a certain basic speed level. But, of course, the longer you have to play at a fast tempo, the harder it is to keep time. It's not only important to reach fast tempos, it is equally important to work on endurance in order to play tight and not to randomly slow down. In this chapter I'll explain how speed and endurance are related to each other and how to improve both.

If this chapter seems too theoretical for you, don't worry. You can just use the "chess field" method of chapter 1 to improve your overall technique, speed, and endurance. Chapters 2 and 3 also provide exercises that automatically improve your playing in terms of speed, endurance, and control. In this chapter, I just want you to understand why your speed improves with certain exercises, while other exercises do not work the same way. With this understanding, you will eventually be able to collect all the exercises necessary to create your individual practice routine.

THE TEMPO FUNCTION—RELATING SPEED AND ENDURANCE

Single-stroke speed and endurance are directly linked, especially when you look at your individual top speed. The individual top speed can be defined as the tempo—measured in beats per minute—you can play for eight bars without a rest. To illustrate this relation less theoretically, let's work with a theoretical example that illustrates a typical, real-life situation:

My drum student, Timmy Gunner, can play alternating sixteenth-note blasts at 180 bpm for eight bars. At anything faster, he can't make it to the end of the eight bars. So 180 bpm is his top speed for single strokes with his hands. The guitarist of his band, Randy Drinkalot, wrote a new song in which the guitar plays eight bars of constant sixteenth-note speed picking throughout the chorus. Now Randy would like Timmy to orchestrate his guitar line with a blast beat. But there's a hitch: The song's original tempo is 190 bpm, a tempo that Timmy isn't able to play yet. However, there's a gig booked in two months and the band would like to play the new song live. So what can Timmy do to play fast enough? To answer that question, it is necessary to learn the basic rules of how speed and endurance are related.

Short-Term vs. Long-Term Speed

You certainly have noticed that at a fast tempo it is easier to play a short 5-stroke roll than to play eight bars of continuous single strokes. So the short-term speed, which I define as sequential notes played for one bar or less (see example 4-1), is usually higher than the long-term speed (eight measures or more). Everything in between one measure and eight measures I call "intermediate speed."

Example 4-1: Short-Term Patterns

I define individual top speed as eight measures of constant single strokes, because it's the "real" speed barrier in extreme metal. Everyone can go fast short-term, but it won't help you to play fast extreme metal songs. To stick to the example, our friend Timmy can reach the desired tempo more effectively by understanding that working on his endurance at slower tempos will also improve his intermediate speed. In a later step, he can turn intermediate speed into top speed.

Timmy's top speed level is 180 bpm, but he also can play sixteen bars at 160 bpm. So our key question is: If he practiced to reach 32 bars at 160 bpm, would it also affect his playing at faster tempos like 180 bpm? **The answer is "yes!"** By increasing his overall endurance to 32 bars at a slower tempo, Timmy also improved his single-stroke technique in general. Thus, he'd probably be able to hit something like twelve to sixteen bars at 180 bpm. Switching to 190 bpm, Jimmy is now probably able to play single strokes for at least four bars (intermediate speed). The method he needs to turn intermediate speed into top speed will be shown later in this chapter. But before we go into detailed exercises, let me sum up the general implications:

If you want to play faster, figure out what your top speed level is and set the metronome to a slower tempo, equal to something like 70 percent of your original top speed. Try to play as many bars as possible and thus increase your endurance. When you go back to the original top speed, you'll notice that playing feels much more comfortable. Once you're able to play at your top speed for longer than eight bars, you can start to raise the tempo. So the basic rule is: The longer you can play something, the faster you can go. This is exactly the way speed and endurance are linked together.

The following sub-chapters will provide basic exercises, which will help you improve both speed and endurance.

Note: Musical Value of Fast Playing
This whole concept might sound very scientific—and it is to a certain degree. However, keep in mind that speed and endurance themselves have no musical value. You can only create musical value by playing fast if the song (or sometimes just a certain part of a song) requires it. Don't play fast just because you can! It's not a sport, not a competition, and you can't win. But you'll certainly lose the audience if you do not connect fast playing with dynamic playing, timing, groove, and the appropriate musical feeling. Likewise, no matter how much you practice on your own, it won't replace the experience you get by playing fast songs with a band. So I strongly recommend starting to play with other musicians. Play challenging songs regularly. In this way you'll improve the most.

INCREASING SINGLE-STROKE ENDURANCE

Hand Exercises

After having basically illustrated this complex topic, it is time to work on specific exercises. Just practicing single strokes on a pad or a snare drum is pretty boring. To make it more interesting and, furthermore, practice things like timing and limb independence and interdependence, use the following exercises. Set the metronome to 70 percent of your individual top speed and just play single strokes with one hand. At the same time, play melodies with the other hand. You can add a foot ostinato on the hi-hat played along with the click track. **Each four-bar phrase must be played eight times!** The goal is to play through the whole exercise without taking a break. It will increase your endurance, thus enhancing your general technique to make you play faster, and it is also a great phrasing exercise.

Exercise 4-2

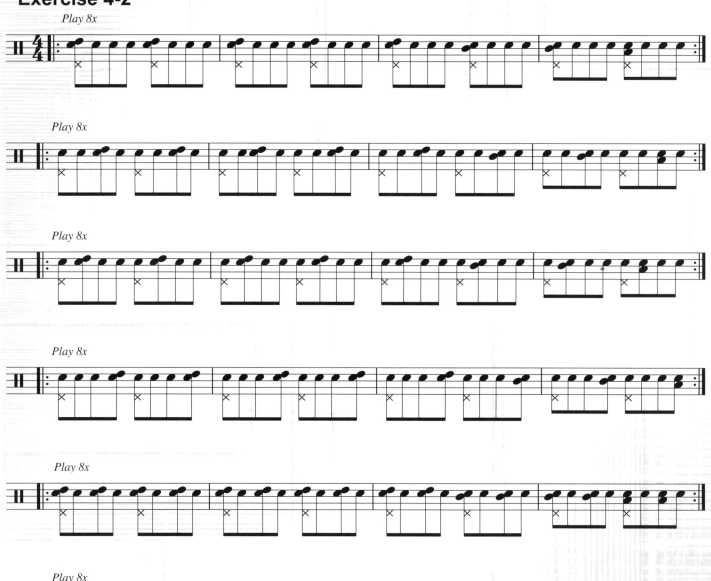

Be creative and develop your own phrases. For that, you can also change the foot pattern when playing melodies and single strokes with your hands. Here are some possibilities (shortened):

Exercise 4-3

Foot Exercises

Set the metronome to a mid-range tempo that equals about 60 to 80 percent of your top speed and play alternating single strokes to a regular 4/4 beat (see exercise 4-4).

Now the length of the single stroke sequence increases in steps of two minutes:

- Do the exercise for two minutes straight, then take a break for one minute.

- Now play alternating single stokes for four minutes, followed by a two-minute break.

- Now play alternating single stokes for six minutes, followed by a three-minute break.

- Now play alternating single stokes for eight minutes, followed by a four-minute break.

- Finally, play alternating single stokes for ten minutes, followed by a five-minute break.

Exercise 4-4

You can use the breaks for doing the hand exercises to save time.

INCREASING SINGLE-STROKE SPEED

Hand exercises

At fast tempos, many drummers have to rely on a certain amount of rebound. Once the rebound changes, perhaps due to playing on a different drumkit, they feel highly irritated and sometimes can't pull off what they could at home on their own gear. There is a really great exercise that helps you drastically increase your single-stroke speed and also get used to different rebounds.

Start with the right hand on the snare drum and play eight bars **at your top speed**. Then play eight bars with the left hand on tom 1, followed by eight bars with the right on tom 2, eight bars with the left on tom 3, and so on. The goal is to play eight bars with each hand on every drum you have. I've got four toms and two snares, which means I'll have to play 96 bars in total (six drums played for eight bars with each hand).

Exercise 4-5

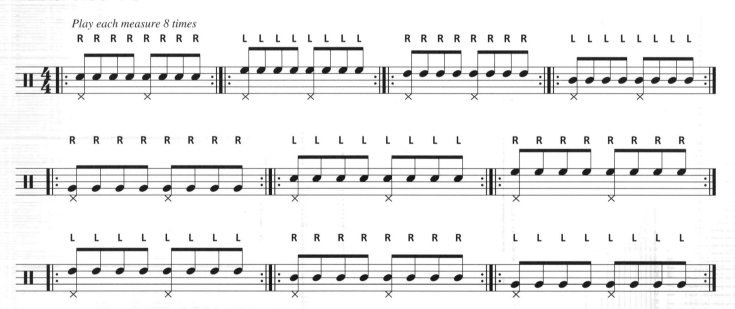

I still need to show you how to turn intermediate speed into top speed with this exercise. The key slogan for that is "two steps forward, one step back!"

To stick to our earlier example, Timmy would play each drum (he has 19 toms and 12 snares) for eight bars at 180 bpm. Now Timmy has to take the next step: If we say that one step is 5 bpm, then Timmy sets his metronome two steps ahead at 190 bpm. Of course, he can't hit the eight bars yet, but Timmy worked hard on his endurance and can play four bars at 190 bpm. After repeating it three times with each hand, he goes back one step and plays at 185 bpm for six bars. Then he goes back to the initial speed of 180 bpm and increases the amount of bars to twelve to sixteen on each drum, playing alternating single strokes. Now, he has to repeat the whole circle **three times.**

There's a mental trick involved: After having played at 190 bpm, going back to 185 bpm doesn't feel as challenging anymore, even though 185 bpm would be the next speed level. But ears and muscles already "got used" to the faster tempo. Timmy's muscles are now ready to hit eight measures at 185 bpm. So Timmy has finally broken his speed barrier and taken the next step.

Here's a general description of how exactly you need to practice exercise 4-5:

- Start at your top speed. Every drum has to be played with each hand separately for eight bars. If you want to apply the exercise to the feet, just play the kick drum with each foot separately.

- Increase the speed level by two steps (one step can be 3, 4, or 5 bpm), and play four bars on every drum, each limb separately. Repeat it three times.

- Decrease the speed by one step and play six to eight bars with each limb separately. Repeat it three times.

- Now go back one step and play twelve to sixteen bars of alternating single strokes at your initial top speed. Repeat it three times.

- Finally, increase the speed by one step again and play alternating single strokes for eight bars.

- Repeat the whole circle three times.

Once you feel comfortable playing eight bars at the next tempo step, you have actually turned intermediate speed into top speed and reached a new top speed level.

Improving Foot Speed

Play single strokes with one foot at your individual top speed for eight bars, and then change the foot. The right hand plays on the ride cymbal or hi-hat; the left hand doesn't play at all. Then play alternating single strokes for eight measures as well, using the same hand pattern. Now, repeat the exercise after thirty seconds of rest, but integrate a snare drum on the "2" and "4." Thus, your point of balance on the drum seat changes. Keeping in balance is very important for your double-kick playing. When you repeat the exercises a third time, lift up the leg that's not playing! This will further improve your balance.

Exercise 4-6

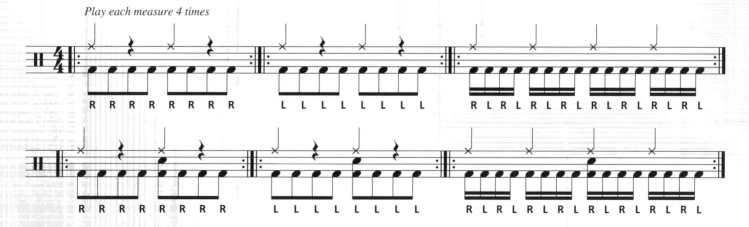

Play each measure 4 times

Now, just like Timmy in the previous example, go two steps further and raise the tempo 10 bpm. Do the exact same exercises, but try to do it for four bars only. You won't be able to reach the eight bars yet. Then go back

5 bpm, which initially would be the next speed level. Now, try to get through the whole eight bars. For the last step, go back to your original top speed and just play alternating single strokes for **more than eight bars**. Repeat the exercise until you reach the next tempo level.

Note: Pedals, Spring Tension, Kick Drum Tuning, Exercise
If another drummer plays fast and uses a certain pedal or a certain tuning, it doesn't mean that the exact same pedal or tuning will do it for you. You need to trust your instinct and use the pedal, tuning, and setup you feel comfortable with immediately. Then you'll have to get used to this one setup. Don't change your sitting position or your spring tension every two weeks, because you'll change the feel for the kick drum and your motion as well. In that case, you would practice with a different motion and not be aware of it! So all the progress you've made with the initial motion is gone. Usually when you make quick progress, there will be moments you feel like you're getting worse again. This is quite normal and happens to everybody. At that point, it would probably be helpful to take a break, maybe one or two days, and let the muscles relax. Oh and by the way, physical exercise is not an equivalent to practice and will not make you play faster or better! Working on your back and stomach muscles, which will help to get a better balance, is a good addition to regular playing, but no substitute for it.

interval Exercises for speed and Endurance

To improve your hand and foot speed you can also use the musical concepts illustrated in chapters 2 and 3. The blast beat perfectly trains your hand speed with alternating single strokes, and the double-bass patterns of chapter 2 can make your feet go faster. Now I'll present some more target-oriented exercises to increase hand and foot speed, as well as endurance.

You need to apply the two-steps-forward method used for exercises 4-5 and 4-6 to each of the following exercises. Just set the metronome to your top speed level and go on from there.

Start with alternating eighth notes on the bass drums, played in a regular 4/4 beat for two bars. Then switch into a blast beat for the same length (see exercise 4-7a). **Repeat the whole exercise a few times without taking a break!**

🔊 **TRACK 19 · 0:00-0:20**

Exercise 4-7a

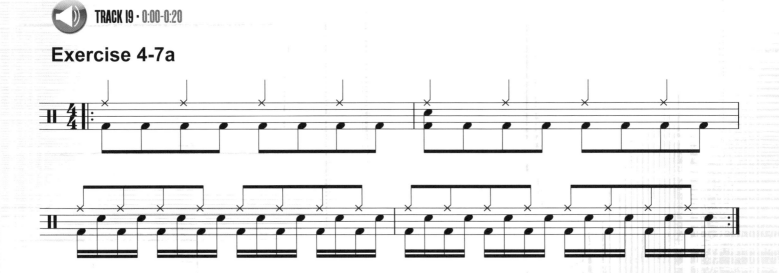

Increase the interval of each section to four bars, played at the same tempo.

Exercise 4-7b

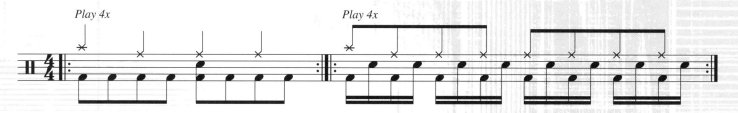

Now, instead of playing eighth notes, play fast sixteenth notes with the feet for two bars.

Exercise 4-7c

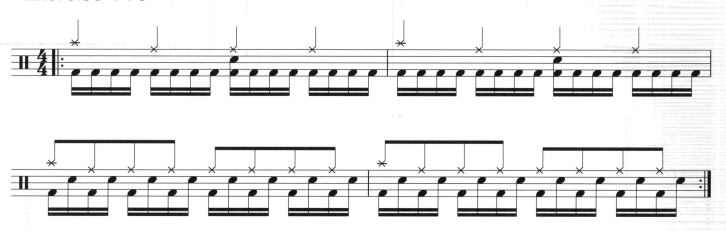

Finally, increase the interval to four bars for each section.

Exercise 4-7d

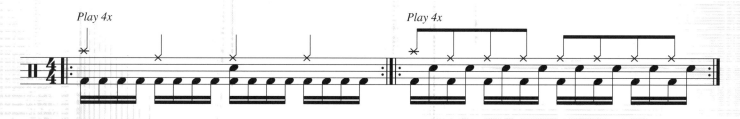

Make sure to play all interval exercises in their entirety at least eight times without stopping!

CHAPTER 5
EXTREME METAL FILLS

There are few musical styles in which the acceptance of playing furious fills is higher than in extreme metal. Many songs need a lot of "dramatic" fills in order to connect one guitar riff with another. This chapter provides some of the hand and foot combinations I find highly useful. Furthermore, you'll learn some of the methods that will enable you to phrase fills diversely.

SIXTEENTH-NOTE ROLLS AND TRIPLET PHRASING

The most common way to orchestrate fills in extreme metal is using fast sixteenth-note snare rolls and tom runs. Typically the phrases are divided into groups of four on each drum, or groups of three with every stroke played on a different drum.

🔊 TRACK 20

Example 5-1

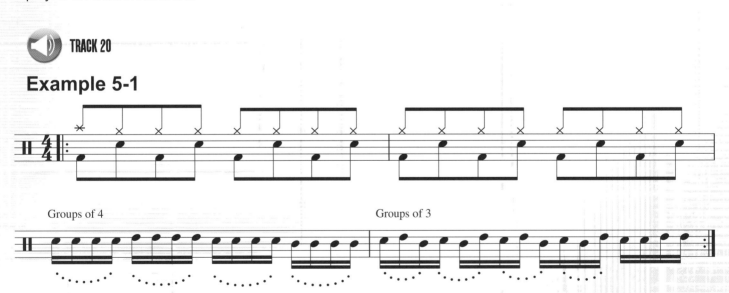

When playing this example it becomes quite obvious that you need a different kind of phrasing in an extreme metal song than, for example, in a funk song, because a fill has to maintain metal's energy and forward-driven character. Also, sixteenth-note snare and tom rolls fit skank beats, blast beats, and fast double-bass grooves very well.

Tom vs. snare placement

You should be aware of the fact that the listener senses every hit on the snare drum as an accent in comparison to the strokes you play on the toms. It can make a huge difference to the overall sound and feel of a fill when changing the snare drum accents and shifting them to other counts. Example 5-2 illustrates how the same rhythmical pattern can be interpreted in three different ways.

 TRACK 21

Example 5-2

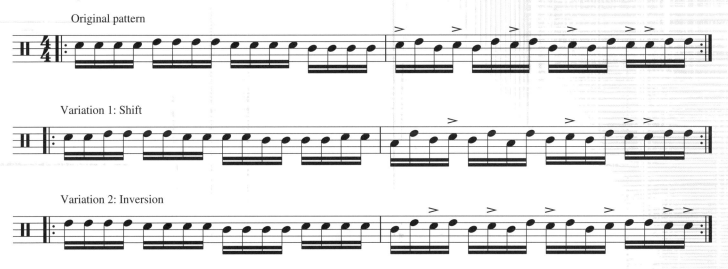

You can also phrase snare/tom rolls as triplets:

 TRACK 22 · 0:00-0:10

Example 5-3a

Now you can combine eighth-note triplets and straight sixteenth notes. Thus, the last bar of example 5-3b sounds even more spectacular and unexpected.

 TRACK 22 · 0:10-0:31

Example 5-3b

It can be very helpful to integrate a pause once in a while. Example 5-4 perfectly illustrates the role of the snare drum as the main fill accent. Before every pause, the subdivision ends on a snare, which sonically creates a surprising upbeat feel.

 TRACK 22 · 0:31-0:54

Example 5-4

An alternative approach to phrase a fill is known as call-and-response. For example, in the breakdown double kick patterns on page 13, you have different groups of eighth and sixteenth notes. These can also be played on toms and snare. By keeping the snare in its initial place and repeating the pattern, you get something like a question-and-answer theme.

 TRACK 23

Example 5-5

Page 13, bar 14

fill exercises

When playing fast sixteenth-note and triplet runs, you can't really go wrong in most genres of extreme metal. But first you need to figure out the sticking for each fill and play it slowly and quietly, to gain the best control possible. After understanding how one pattern works, integrate the fill into a groove, which is the best way to refine newly developed fill phrasings. These exercises work with three toms, but you can also extend the patterns on a bigger drumkit.

LINEAR HAND/FOOT COMBINATIONS

The following exercises feature a very common way of playing fills. Typically you play groups of two or four alternating sixteenth notes with the hands, followed by two kicks. These exercises usually emerge from linear eighth-note patterns broken up between right hand and right foot. By doubling the amount of strokes, first by feet, then also by hands, you can create fast rhythmical sixteenth-note patterns, which fit very well with blast beats and fast double-bass drumming.

 TRACK 24

Example 5-6

Of course, it is also possible to integrate triplets into these linear hand/foot combinations. Here's an example:

 TRACK 25

Example 5-7a

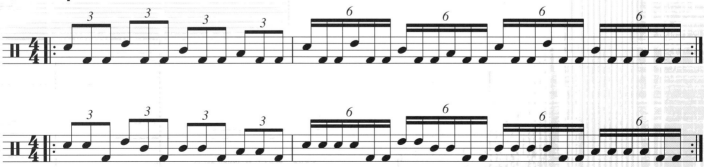

Depending on where you put the snare drum, the sound of the whole pattern changes:

Example 5-7b

It is also very common to play an equal number of notes with hands and feet—for example, four notes with hands followed by four notes with feet, etc.

Example 5-8a

Sometimes the kick drums are played in unison with the right hand on the ride cymbal and the left hand on the hi-hat.

Example 5-8b

Instead of playing a regular linear pattern, you can invert the pattern—for example, starting with your feet instead of the hands. In the linear-fill exercises on the next page, in each line the first measure shows the original idea, and the second measure is its mirror image. Again, first practice the pattern itself slowly and quietly, and bring it up to the desired tempo later by integrating it into a groove.

Linear Fill Exercises

Linear Triplet Fill Exercises

PART II

MUSICAL APPLICATION

CHAPTER 6
EXTREME METAL GROOVE STUDIES

Just like the terms *technique* or *feeling,* the term *groove* seems to be something that every drummer knows by instinct. However, many drummers use the word *groove* in the same way to name one specific, very concrete beat variation (for example, the shuffle "groove" in the Toto song "Rosanna") and to describe a certain overall emotion that music provides ("this drummer has a phenomenal groove!"). So it is not a well-defined term that everybody understands in the same way. I don't want to get into the different varieties of how to feel a groove in general, because with this topic, one could fill another whole book. Instead, in this chapter, I want to demonstrate some of the conceptual groove variations (and being very concrete with it) that occur in extreme metal music, and just go a little into the different ways of possibly interpreting it dynamically.

CONCEPTUAL DRUMSET VARIATIONS

For developing specific groove ideas, a helpful concept is to look at different components of your drumset first and use a certain drum or cymbal as main tool to develop an idea musically. After all, every drum and cymbal is a single instrument and can lead your groove. Below you'll find some conceptions about the single instruments and their interpretation when applied for extreme metal grooves. For all examples shown here, keep in mind that repetition is a very important factor of groove playing, because if you do not repeat a phrase, the listener will not be able to recognize it.

ride cymbal variations

The first conceptual piece of the drumset we look at is the ride cymbal. Example 6-1a illustrates a very basic, but typical, pattern that is frequently used in extreme metal, especially in thrash metal, from which it emerged. The pattern is basically a regular 4/4 with kick drums on the downbeats (1 and 3), and the snare on the upbeats (2 and 4). The ride cymbal is playing on all sixteenth-note subdivisions. Being the leading force of the groove, it should be played with the intention to sound "heavy" and to cut through. One prominent drummer who uses these kinds of grooves extensively is Dave Lombardo, who even managed to make these ride patterns become basic drum knowledge for all extreme metal drummers who came after him. Typical examples of Lombardo's approach to ride playing are the Slayer songs "Criminally Insane" and "South of Heaven," or the song "Rusty Nail" by Grip Inc.

TRACK 28

Example 6-1a

Example 6-1b shows another typical ride variation. By keeping the steady sixteenth notes on the ride and playing the kick and the snare half-time, you can slow the pace of a song without losing its original drive or changing the basic tempo. In this variation, any additional bass or snare hit can make a huge change to the groove, as you can tell when executing a little snare, kick, and crash syncopation throughout the exercise.

TRACK 29

Example 6-1b

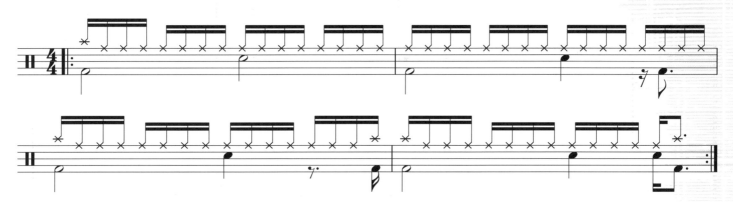

A very typical variation in songwriting would be to switch from the half-time feel into the straight feel of example 6-1a, which resolves the musical suspense and drives the song forward. There is no change of the tempo itself, but the listener gets the impression that the song's tempo is tightening up. Listen to example 6-1c and try to evaluate what the change of pace implies to you emotionally.

TRACK 30

Example 6-1c

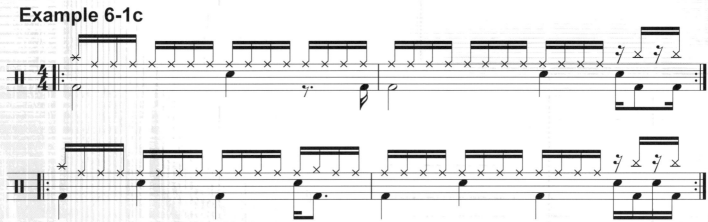

Of course, you can apply the same groove concept to a 12/8 or a 4/4 triplet groove. Examples 6-2a and b show different notations of the same basic feel, always subdividing the beat into groups of three. When you combine this new phrasing with example 6-1, you'll notice that in the first example the ride stays the same while kick and snare syncopate and thus make the pace become slower. In the second example, kick and snare stay on the same counts and the ride becomes faster.

TRACK 31

Example 6-2a: Ride Maintains Its Tempo

Example 6-2b: Ride Increases Its Tempo

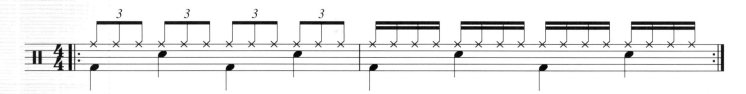

Now you can play some variations of the ride pattern. In example 6-3 you'll find one pattern that typically works.

TRACK 32

Example 6-3

A more advanced way of phrasing is shown in example 6-4. Here you have a repeated phrase consisting of a sixteenth note followed by a thirty-second-note double stroke on the ride followed by a snare note. The double stroke is played with the right hand only, which makes the pattern technically challenging.

Example 6-4

It is very common to execute ride cymbal and bass drums in unison, even when playing faster patterns. Examples 6-5a and b illustrate typical variations. Mostly the thirty-second-note subdivisions are played between two rides, or between the right hand on the ride and the left hand on an additional bell. The same goes for triplets in example b. In general, you can apply this kind of ride playing to all the double-bass exercises of chapter 2 as well.

Example 6-5a

Example 6-5b

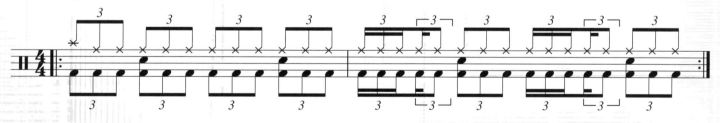

Of course, you can also apply ride cymbal playing to skank beats. Example 6-6 shows some variations, which are more difficult than the previous examples and need to be practiced very slowly at first to get your hands and feet in sync.

TRACK 36

Example 6-6

Aggressive open Hi-Hat beats

Instead of using the ride cymbal, you can base your grooves on the hi-hat. However, you will rarely find a closed hi-hat being used like it is in funk or pop music. To provide the listener with a more raw and aggressive feel, play powerful strokes on an open hi-hat. This way of playing the hi-hat, which directly influenced later metal drumming, evolved from the hard rock and early heavy metal drumming of the late 1960s and early '70s. Famous examples can be found in John Bonham's (Led Zeppelin) "Rock and Roll" and "The Song Remains the Same," Bill Ward's (Black Sabbath) "War Pigs," or Ian Paice's (Deep Purple) "Highway Star" and "Burn" playing. Even some jazz drummers used this hi-hat style as well; one famous example is Tony Williams (Lifetime) in "Snake Oil."

Example 6-7 shows a typical modern, thrashy, open hi-hat groove, played in two different time feels. Listen to the track on the CD to get a good impression of what the example really sounds like. This notation comes as close as possible to the sound of its original interpretation.

TRACK 37

Example 6-7

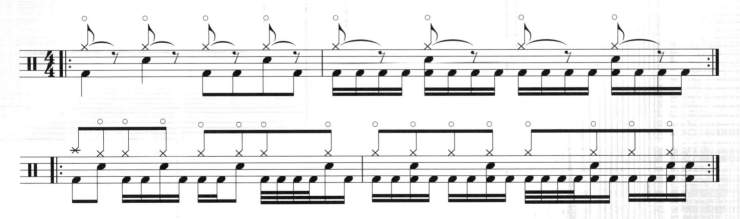

Basically you can apply all exercises in this book to open hi-hat playing. And whatever you play on the open hi-hat might also work very well on crash, splash, or China cymbals. Here are some variations:

Example 6-8

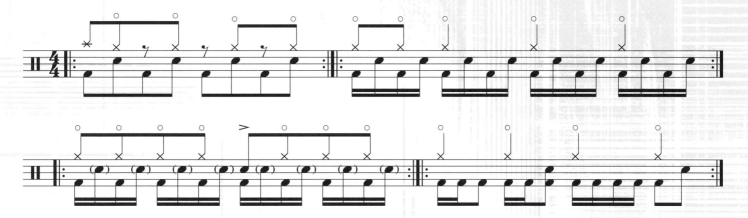

Leading Tom Grooves

Toms are not just for playing fills; they play a leading role in many metal grooves. The first example of a heavy metal song I can think of in which the toms played a leading role in the groove is Blue Cheer's version of "Summertime Blues" (1968). The song's drum line could be seen as a role model for how the toms were approached later on in metal drumming. Referring to this classic song, example 6-9 shows two tom grooves, which are very similar to the way they were first used.

Example 6-9

In modern extreme metal drumming, this way of using toms hasn't changed that much stylistically, just the overall technicality and speed of the music have evolved. One big difference between normal rock drumming and metal drumming is the use of double-bass drumming for playing tom grooves.

TRACK 40

Example 6-10

Just like applying different phrasings to ride playing (see example 6-8), you can generally apply all patterns you've learned so far to the toms as well. The following example gives you an idea.

 TRACK 41

Example 6-11

The Role of Snare and Bass Drum

If you analyze the role of snare and bass drum in the previous examples, it should be pretty obvious that in extreme metal drumming, both components mostly operate as one unit to define the accents of a groove. A heavy downbeat bass drum accent ("call") waits for its heavy upbeat snare counterpoint ("response"), so to speak. So both instruments act in the same way as a modern rock drummer would approach them. But typically the placement of extreme metal kick and snare accents is a little more wild, syncopated, and less steady.

Note: Time

Groove and time feel are strongly related to each other. In Gary Chester's famous book The New Breed, *the author differentiates between three basic time feels, which are standard in modern music: "on top," "in the middle," and "behind." For extreme metal all these different time feels apply as well. You'll just find more drummers that generally play "on top" of the beat, which means playing slightly ahead of the actual metronomic quarter-note pulse. This provides a frantic, energetic feel, but you have to be careful not to rush. Fast stuff always sounds best in this genre when played "in the middle," which means as close to the metronomic grid as possible, with every stroke having mathematically the right length in correlation to another. A good example of this mathematical time feel are the albums* Epitaph *by the band Necrophagist and* Nocturnal *by The Black Dahlia Murder. Playing "behind" or laid-back is rarely found in extreme metal music. Check out* Focus *by the band Cynic and their drummer Sean Reinert, who mastered playing laid-back grooves within a metal context. Another example for playing in a laid-back feel is the Swiss/German band Triptykon.*

ADAPTING DYNAMICS TO GIVEN STYLES AND PHRASINGS

When playing a song, it is one of the drummer's main tasks to create and release tension. This can be done by varying the dynamic parameters of a song, which are tempo, time, volume, and the amount of notes played. Many extreme metal songs start with a certain musical idea—typically a guitar riff. In some cases a rhythmical pattern can also be the starting point for creating original material. In all cases you'll have to work out phrases and accents in order to make the music groove. But since a drummer has to control the dynamic progression and thus the song's arc of suspense, you'll somehow have to deal most creatively and carefully with being bound to a certain riff. In this section I've collected some of the main examples showing how drum grooves can be connected with specific given musical ideas, how they typically appear in extreme metal, and how to adapt a song's dynamic progression by changing the drum groove itself.

playing to a syncopated guitar groove

In syncopated guitar riffs, the notes do not fall on straight quarter- (or eighth-) note counts. Instead, the guitar plays in subdivisions off the regular counts. There are two syncopated guitar riffs on the included CD (track 42) that could be rhythmically transcribed like this:

 TRACK 42

Example 6-12: Guitar Riff 1 and 2 Rhythmically

One approach to make riff 1 groove (now I'm referring to "groove" as an emotional aspect in music) is to create a counterpart to the guitar line and play on all even quarter-note counts. This provides a very powerful and heavy feel. In example 6-12a, the hi-hat and snare remain on the even quarter-note beats, but the kick drum plays in unison with the guitars. Thus you can have both, creating a rhythmical counterpart and underlining the original guitar groove.

TRACK 43 · 83 (PLAY-ALONG)

Example 6-12a

In example 6-12b, you can hear what happens to the riff if you phrase all syncopated accents in sync with the guitar. The groove loses its clarity, which in certain situations can be an advantage or a disadvantage, depending on which direction the song is going and how you want to create tension with the drums.

 TRACK 44 · 83 (PLAY-ALONG)

Example 6-12b

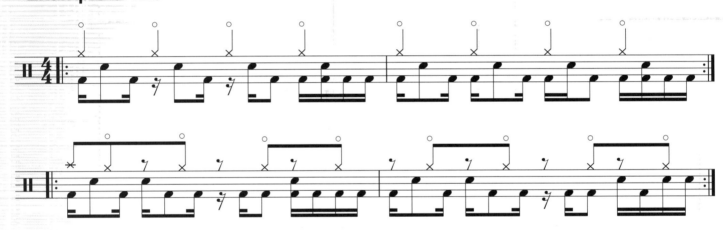

Speaking of creating and releasing tension, example 6-13a perfectly illustrates how to increase tension by changing the resolution of single drumset components. Along with guitar riff 2, the drums play a basic sixteenth-note double-kick backbeat, with quarter-note accents on the open hi-hat and the snare played on 2 and 4. As you can see, the groove component "hi-hat" just changes its resolution from quarter to eighth notes, which creates a more forward-driven feel. The pattern is just interspersed with a group of four thirty-second notes and one sixteenth note, which is exactly the kind of 5-roll-phrasing you learned in chapter 2. Also, the snare plays a little variation at the end. By playing this variation, the musical tension can be increased by just making a small adjustment. The change from the hi-hat to the ride bell makes the groove sound more intense and provides more overall variety.

TRACK 45 · 84 (PLAY-ALONG)

Example 6-13a

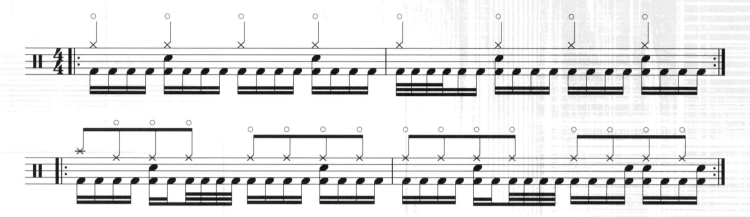

Even though repetition is important for groove playing, sometimes you need an element of surprise to make the song more interesting. Example 6-13b illustrates a totally different way of accompanying guitar riff 2. By decoupling the groove's syncopation from the riff's original accents, the listener will be "confused," but in a good way; since the listener does not know how the song will further evolve, he remains curious.

TRACK 46 · 84 (PLAY-ALONG)

Example 6-13b

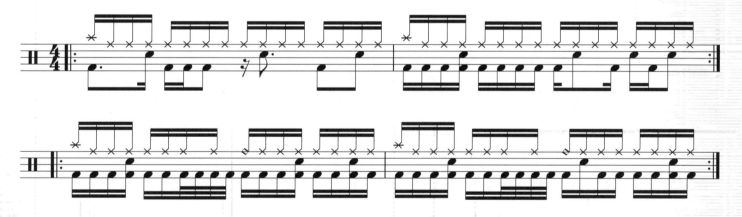

Now it's time to put together all parts previously learned. In example 6-14 you see one way to connect both guitar riffs with a drum fill. In the third bar of this example the toms adapt the new phrasing of riff 2 while still accompanying riff 1. Thus, you introduce the listener to the next part and lead into riff 2 logically by using its accents. After having built up tension, you need to resolve it and let the riff find its final "flow." Similar to the previous examples, in which tension was built up by changing the resolution of one groove component, you now can also change the resolution of snare and hi-hat at once and change the time feel to double-time (eighth bar of this example). Thus the groove gets more drive and also feels faster. At the end, ongoing thirty-second notes are played on the bass drum, which means another augmentation of musical intensity. After all, fast playing does make sense musically when integrating it into a song's dynamic structure.

On the CD you can find example 6-14 in the middle section of song example 3 (track 92).

Example 6-14

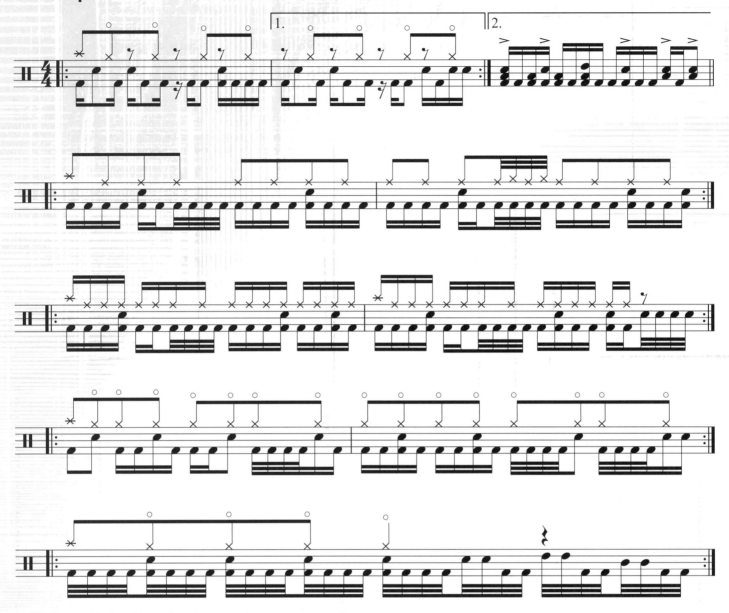

Playing to a speed-picked guitar riff

In extreme metal, the guitars often play speed-picked guitar riffs, which have a large amount of ongoing sixteenth notes in them, similar to the blast or fast double-bass drumming. When playing at a fast tempo, it doesn't mean that groove isn't important—or even worse, that it isn't supposed to be there. The starting point to shape the right groove is the basic quarter-note pulse on the counts 1 – 2 – 3 – 4. However, when the guitarist is fast picking, the quarter-note pulse can be difficult to find at times. So the first thing you need to find out is whether the guitar picks a binary pulse (quarter, eighth, sixteenth, and thirty-second notes) or a ternary pulse (all sorts of triplets). Then logically you need to adapt to this kind of phrasing. For instance, when drums play straight sixteenth notes but the guitar plays sixteenth-note triplets at the same time, it is impossible to generate a groove the listener can feel or identify. So make sure that guitars, bass, and drums are in sync.

There are many possibilities to accompany a speed-picked guitar riff. One way is to play grooves similar to the ones used previously and see if they fit (see example 6-15a). It is very likely a much better choice to stick to a binary note resolution, especially with the kicks. Triplets will disturb the groove feel.

 TRACK 47 · 85 (PLAY-ALONG)

Example 6-15a

It seems obvious that it might be a better musical fit to somehow keep up with the fast picking of the guitars. Therefore, you have different options, depending on your technical level of playing. In example 6-15b, the bass drums are adapting to the sixteenth notes of the guitar. This is a very typical example of how to comp a speed-picked riff effectively.

 TRACK 48, 49 · 85 (PLAY-ALONG)

Example 6-15b

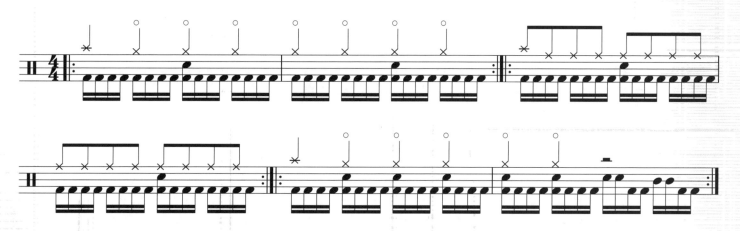

You can also accompany the guitar line by playing skank beats, which technically makes it a little easier for you. In example 6-15c a skank beat, and later a reversed skank beat, are interspersed by a few sixteenth notes, which help to underline the riff's fast character.

TRACK 50 · 85 (PLAY-ALONG)

Example 6-15c

The same principles can be applied to triplets. In example 6-16 you'll find all sorts of basic triplet interpretations. Every new interpretation is repeated once. In this way you could also build up a drum part for a song. You can hear a very similar way of triplet playing in song example 2 (track 90).

Example 6-16

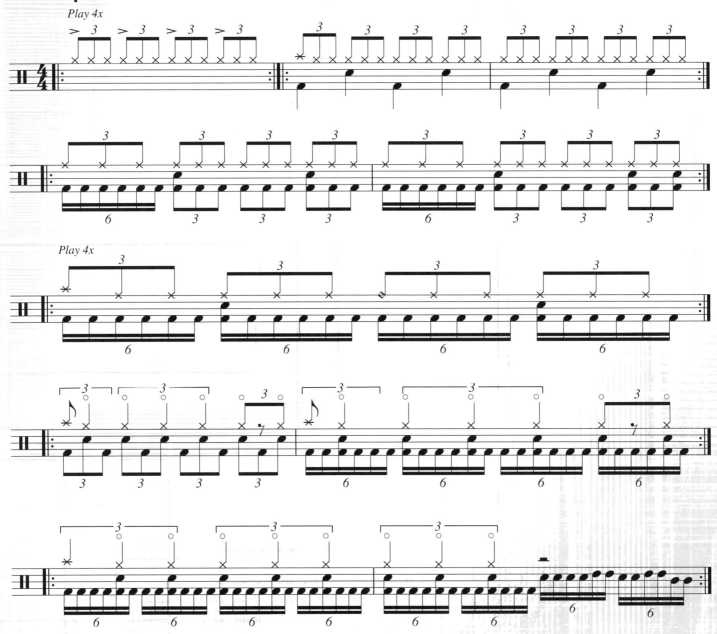

Accompanying Doom and Sludge Riffs

Even though this book is largely about speed and fast playing, you can also find the complete opposite in extreme metal music. The main characteristics of so-called genres like "doom metal" and "sludge" are a slow tempo and low-tuned instruments to provide the heaviest feel possible. These sub-genres evolved from 1970s music that also was played slowly and sounded extremely heavy for the time, with bands like Pentagram and, of course, Black Sabbath. The music and its characteristics finally survived and found their way into the extreme metal community.

For these sub-genres the most important skill of a drummer isn't his technical ability. He must also be able to play the right accents at the right time with a necessary laid-back, heavy feel, and also lead the band in slow parts by playing accurately. With guitars being heavily distorted, sloppiness just creates noise, not musical impact! So when playing slow tempos, it is even more important to have a good time feel and to play tight as a band, because the space in between each subdivision is huge compared to fast stuff. At the same time, there is a lot of room for playing heavy tom fills and accents.

Example 6-17 shows the drum line for a possible doom metal riff. It always fits to work with heavy ride and crash cymbals, open hi-hats, and low floor toms. The snare on count 2 is played as a flam to additionally underline its role as the center of the groove.

 TRACK 51

Example 6-17

Sometimes in extreme metal, a slow riff is accompanied by slow hands combined with fast feet. When integrating faster ongoing double-bass playing into "slow-motion" grooves, hands need to maintain long note values in order to preserve the slow groove feel. Usually, faster double-bass drumming is used only after the riff has further progressed, which is beneficial for increasing the musical tension. Example 6-18 shows a typical way of progressing a doom riff. Don't be afraid of the thirty-second notes; the tempo is only 70 bpm.

Example 6-18

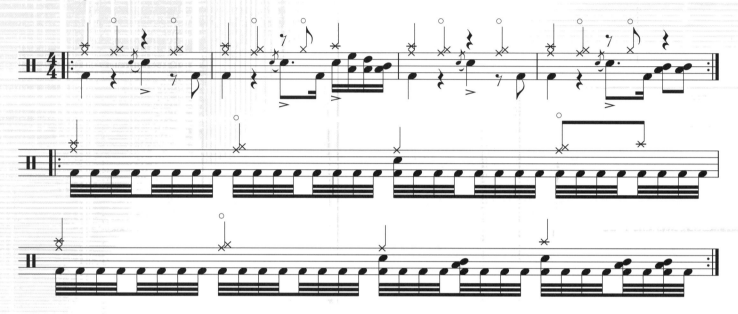

CHAPTER 7
EXPLORING THE MUSICAL USE OF BLAST BEATS

When you have invested time in pulling off blast beat exercises and practicing speed and technique, you naturally want to use these skills in a band context. Therefore, you need to understand how to adapt phrasing, dynamics, and accents to different musical situations, and how blasts work together with other possible groove concepts. After having learned the most important phrases, accents, and techniques in chapter 3, this chapter explains a few specific examples of how to use blast beats musically for all subgenres of extreme metal.

MUSICAL MEANING: WHY, WHEN, AND HOW TO INTERPRET BLASTS DYNAMICALLY

There are different types of blast beats (see page 17) and various ways of phrasing them (see page 23), merely depending on the note value. You can also interpret the role of a blast beat according to the dynamic context in which the beat occurs. To give a blast beat value and meaning, there is one question that needs to be answered first: When do you choose to play a blast beat?

Being a drummer, usually someone in your band throws a certain musical idea (like a guitar riff) at you, and now you need to come up with a drum beat that fits best. On the included CD you can find a typical extreme metal guitar riff (track 52). To find out how a blast beat feels with such a riff, compare the blast to a standard 4/4 backbeat (see example 7-1). Both beats project distinct musical identities—the basic 4/4 groove is a general pop music component, the blast beat a typical element in extreme metal music. So the standard 4/4 beat provides a whole different feel compared to the blast. It is your job to find out in which direction to drag a certain riff.

TRACK 52 · 86 (PLAY-ALONG)

Example 7-1

So, to decide if a riff needs a blast beat, you must assess if the blast beat best supports the riff's musical character. This, of course, is a matter of taste and feeling and should be valued individually, but some riffs just typically fit with blast beats, whereas other riffs just don't.

At the same time, the impact of a blast beat depends on the song structure in which the beat occurs. So after having figured out the musical character of one specific idea, you need to have a vision about the role a blast beat riff could play in the song context. Here are three possibilities:

1. The blast is used in a main riff of the song, for instance in a chorus riff.

2. The blast is used only sporadically and unexpectedly.

3. The blast is used constantly throughout most parts of the song.

The first mode is the clearest way to interpret a blast beat musically. When you use the blast beat for the main riff or leading theme in a song, all other rhythmical ideas sort of lead towards the main blast riff, especially when playing it in a chorus (even though extreme metal music often doesn't work with traditional songwriting structures). So in this example, the blast has a priority role.

The second mode is a little more difficult to approach. When a blast is meant to be unexpected and thus surprise the listener, you need to play it with even more power and conviction, because the blast then, most likely, constitutes the peak level of energy. Then it is also most important to find ways (i.e., grooves and beats) to logically lead to the blast in the most suspenseful manner.

In mode 3, the blast beat has a totally different role. It just keeps a steady pulse, and so all other grooves and phrases used in the song stand out more. Sometimes, especially in black metal music, blast beats are used to create a kind of musical monotony. The specific task for this way of interpretation is to wrap up the listener in the overall "wall of sound" created by the blast and the riff together. The guitar riffs used here usually sound very different from riffs that would work for modes 2 and 3.

Before illustrating these three modes with actual examples, there is one basic piece missing. The last question to be found in the previous section about "how" to play a blast is connected with the questions about why and when to play blasts. "How" refers to its dynamic interpretation and in which way the blast is played, and "what" means how hard you hit and what cymbals you chose. This dynamic interpretation is based on exactly how the guitar riff is composed. Here are the two most typical ways:

1. The riff has a staccato feel with a lot of eighth-note accents and syncopation. In this case, the drums adapt to the guitar riff by playing staccato accents on a cymbal. The snare drum is played powerfully to build the counterpart to the kick drums, with some sort of machine-gun-like attack. This kind of dynamic interpretation is typically used for sporadic blast riffs (modes 1 and 2 above).

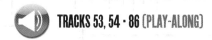

TRACKS 53, 54 · 86 (PLAY-ALONG)

Example 7-2

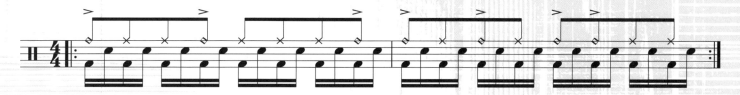

2. The riff has a legato feel and many long, open notes in it. Look at example 7-3 and notice how the drums adapt to the legato feel by using an almost opened hi-hat. The snare drum is no longer a counterpart to the kick drums; it's more like some sort of additional sound source resembling the hi-hat. This way of interpretation primarily applies to mode 3, when the blast is used throughout most parts of a song.

TRACK 55

Example 7-3

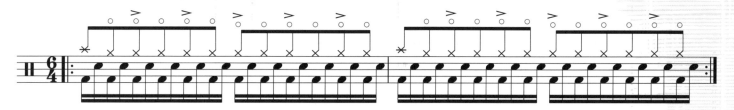

In this mode, backbeat blasts work very well. Of course, you can also use non-alternating bomb or gravity blasts to play these examples. In this section I decided only to work with traditional blasts since the fundamental principles shown here can be applied to other kinds of blasts as well.

Finding the Right Tempo

I recommend playing blasts at tempos over 170 bpm, since a certain speed definitely can increase the musical intensity. But at the same time, if the tempo is *too* fast, the blast can lose its entire music relevance. Record yourself and listen to all your ideas at slow and fast tempos. It will give you an impression about how tempo can change the character of a riff.

Applying Blasts to Different Musical Situations

Regarding our three different modes, it is now important to connect the blast beat with other grooves and beat concepts and make it work within a song. The following examples are just a few obvious ways of how to create a certain desired musical feel. There are many more possibilities of how to connect blast beats with other groove concepts, but there is no general rule about how it works. You'll have to be creative and find out for yourself.

1. The blast is used in a main riff of the song, like for instance in a chorus riff. Since the blast itself is a very forward driven type of beat, it usually makes sense to use other forward driven beat concepts to connect with the main blast riff. In example 7-4 you see something typical for extreme metal songwriting. First, the riff kicks in with a skank beat that turns into a blast. With the blast beat being a double-time skank beat, combining both concepts is usually a perfect match. Watch the right hand's cymbal accents; they're maintained when playing the blast.

 **TRACK 56**

Example 7-4

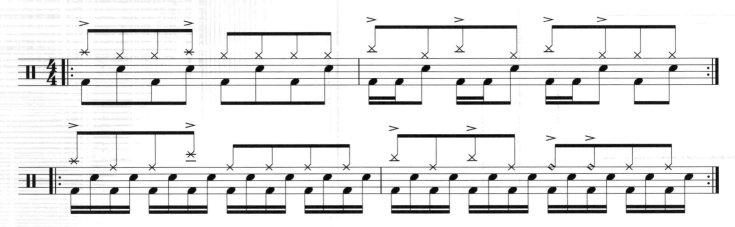

In examples 7-5a and 7-5b you get an impression how the same idea works with reversed skank beats and a steady double-bass groove. Notice what a huge impact a little fill can have when leading into the blast part!

 **TRACK 57**

Example 7-5a

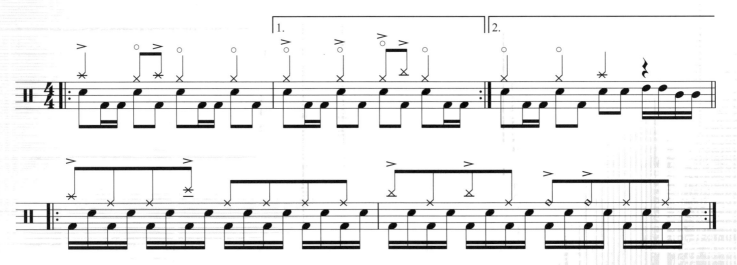

TRACK 58

Example 7-5b

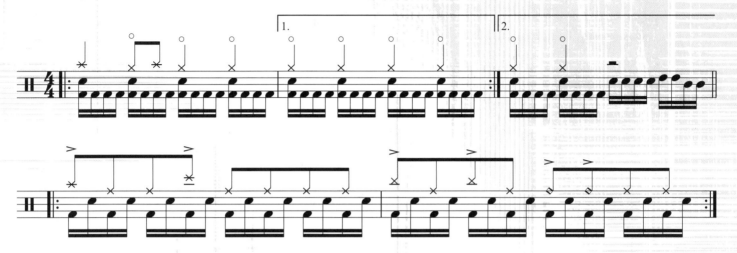

2. The blast is used only sporadically and unexpectedly. In this situation, the musical tension needs to be maximized before playing the blast beat, which happens by creating a strong contrast. There are different ways to do that. One very obvious way would be working with rests, as the musical contrast between playing a lot of notes in the blast and not playing at all is evident. Example 7-6a works with a quarter-note rest before the blast kicks in.

 TRACK 59

Example 7-6a

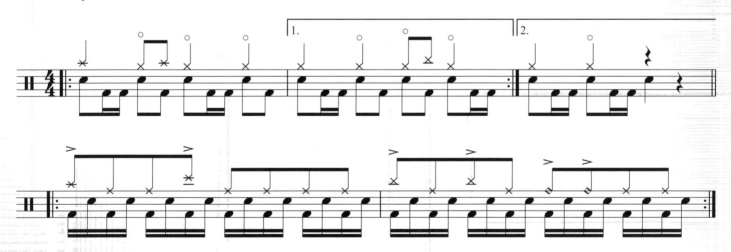

Often it fits very well to rest for three beats and then play a single, very loud snare accent on the last quarter note (see example 7-6 b), or even play a fast intro fill (example 7-6c).

TRACK 60

Example 7-6b

TRACK 61

Example 7-6c

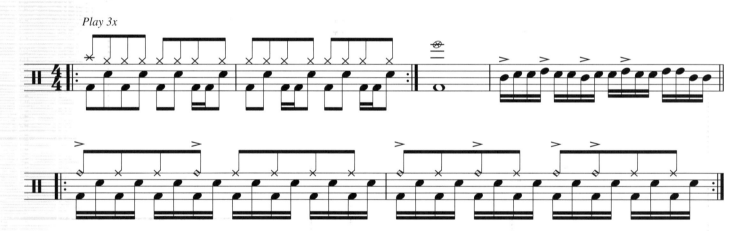

A special case of building up musical intensity is shown in example 7-7. There's a four-bar intro right before the blast, in which the note values become slightly shorter and shorter. Thus, the listener has the impression that the tempo also becomes faster and faster. In fact, the tempo remains the same. At the end, the blast beat has the fastest note resolution and, thus, the musical tension is finally relieved.

Example 7-7

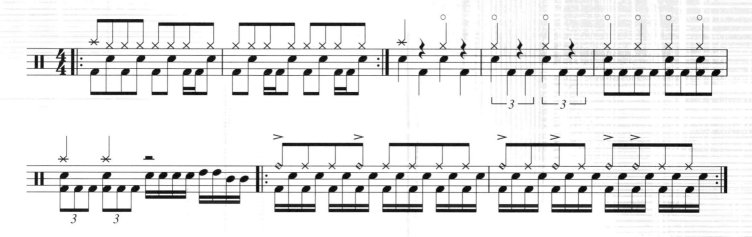

3. The blast is used constantly throughout most parts of the song. In this case, anything can work to help distinguish between different song sections. Usually a good method is to alternate hi-hat and ride cymbal from part to part. Constant blasting can be very tiring, so use some fills or other beats to take a rest once a while.

Example 7-8

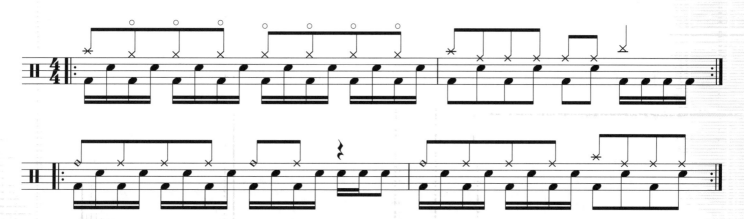

SPECIFIC APPROACHES TO PHRASING BLAST BEATS WITHIN A RIFF CONTEXT

Thus far in this chapter, you have learned many different possibilities in order to understand the whole musical concept of the blast beat and how to use it in a song context. Now it is necessary to delve a little deeper into the different possibilities of phrasing a blast beat when accompanying an individual riff.

phrasing along the riff's melody

The previous examples were based on two main components of songwriting: structure and dynamics. Other components are melody, harmonics, time, tempo, and rhythm. Of course, for a drummer, the harmonic approach is not too relevant, with the drums being a rhythmic instrument. But a great starting point is to figure out the melody of a guitar line and to phrase the ride cymbal along with the higher notes of the riff. Example 7-9 illustrates the rhythmical pattern of the riff, with all high accents played on the ride bell.

Example 7-9

These accents are now played by the ride cymbal in a triplet blast beat phrasing (see example 7-9a). By referring to the guitar accents, you stick to the riff's melodic structure, which means that you have found a melodic approach to utilizing blast beats. The blast is played traditionally first and then turns into a non-alternating variation.

 TRACK 62 · 87 (PLAY-ALONG)

Example 7-9a

Example 7-9b proves that the same accents also work when playing a bomb blast. The accents are now played by the left hand on a China cymbal.

Example 7-9b

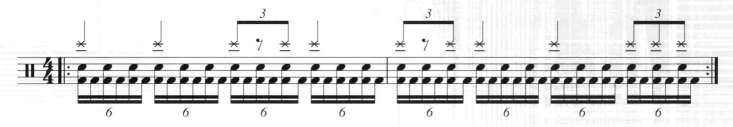

phrasing against the riff's melody

Another possibility to accompany a riff is to syncopate its accents, thereby creating some sort of question-answer theme with drums and guitars. In example 7-10a all ride accents of pattern 7-9a are shifted.

Example 7-10a

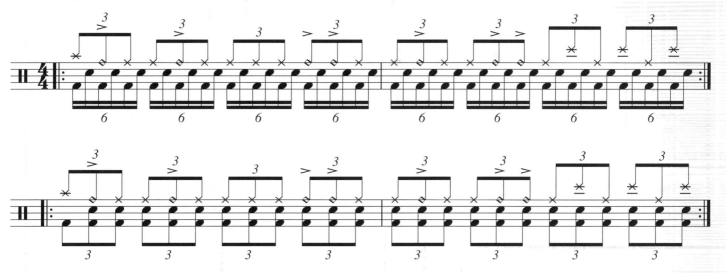

This works with bomb blasts as well.

Example 7-10b

using a Fixed rhythmic unit to phrase blasts

Now we will consider another possible component of songwriting, which is rhythm. Of course, for any drummer, rhythm is the main field to express oneself musically. To tell you that I use rhythmical approaches for the drums is like saying a mathematician uses numbers or a writer uses words. I would like to go into a few detailed rhythmical examples showing that sometimes it makes sense to stick to one rhythmic pattern when accompanying a riff. This is the case especially when all guitars aren't clearly audible in a live situation. All your bandmates need is a rhythmical compass they can rely on. When playing a blast beat, the only way to lead is by using cymbal accents.

In example 7-11a you'll find a typical 3-2 clave phrase. This phrase can also be transferred into steady eighth notes by keeping the accents.

🔊 **TRACK 63 · 0:00-0:20**

Example 7-11a

Now you can apply these accents to the right hand on the ride cymbal and playing kick drums underneath.

🔊 **TRACK 63 · 0:20-0:35**

Example 7-11b

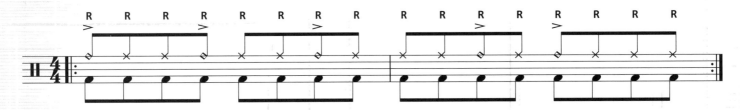

To create a blast beat with the clave phrasing you only need to integrate the left hand on the snare. Also listen to the track on the CD and compare it to the other two examples. This gives you another option for how to find the best drum line for a certain riff.

TRACK 64

Example 7-11c

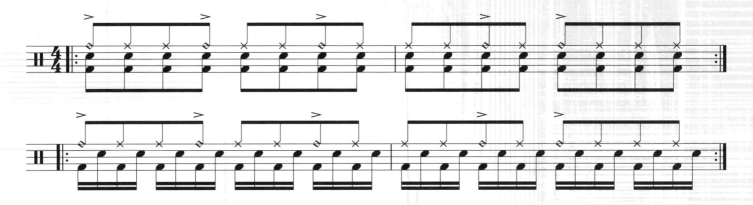

The same approach works for any other fixed rhythmic concept. Another example, this time in 12/8, is the Buleria, a rhythm that is used in Flamenco music. The main pulse is written out in example 7-12a. The Buleria works for blast accents very well because it consists of ongoing eighth notes.

TRACK 65 · 0:00-0:12

Example 7-12a: Buleria: Basic Pattern

Now integrate kick drums and left hand on the snare.

TRACK 65 · 0:12-0:51

Example 7-12b

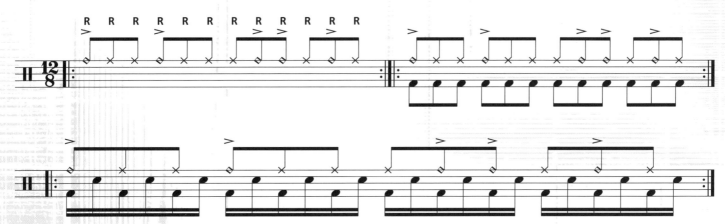

odd-Time Blasts

The key to clarifying a certain phrasing or musical idea rhythmically is to use accents. By the use of accents, the idea becomes rhythmically shaped, and the listener can hear a distinct pattern instead of just fast random notes. This basic musical "law" becomes even more important when a blast beat comes in an odd-meter grouping.

Example 7-13a is a typical 5/4 phrasing dividing groups of five eighth notes in groups of two and three, counting 1-2-1-2-3 instead of 1-2-3-4-5. Every "1" is accented:

 TRACK 66 · 0:00-0:06

Example 7-13a

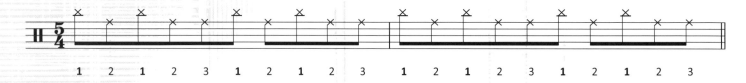

Now it is possible to interpret this phrasing as a blast beat, which we see in example 7-13b.

 TRACK 66 · 0:06-0:40

Example 7-13b

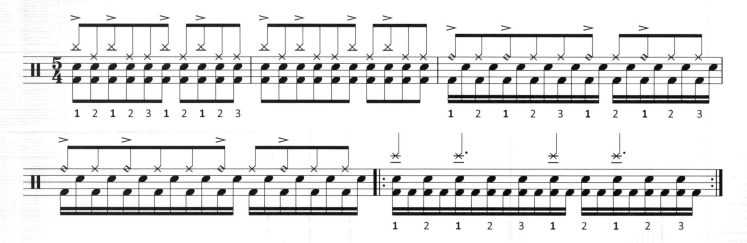

You can also invert the pattern and count **1**-2-3-**1**-2:

 TRACK 67

Example 7-13c

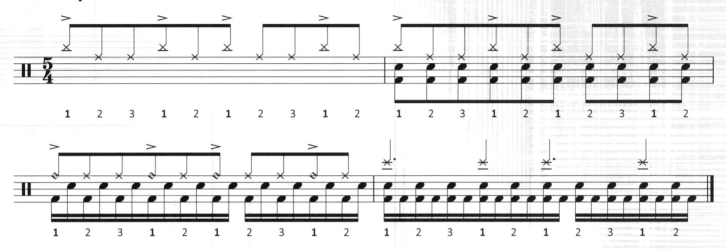

The principle of subdividing odd-time signatures into smaller rhythmic groups is very practical and automatically shapes an accented phrase that—by repetition—becomes a groove. Here's an example in 7/4. The seven eighth notes are divided into two groups of two eighth notes and one group of three eighth notes, like **1**-2-**1**-2-**1**-2-3:

 TRACK 68 · 0:00-0:07

Example 7-14a

Now use the same pattern for accenting the blast in 7/4:

 TRACK 68 · 0:07-0:46

Example 7-14b

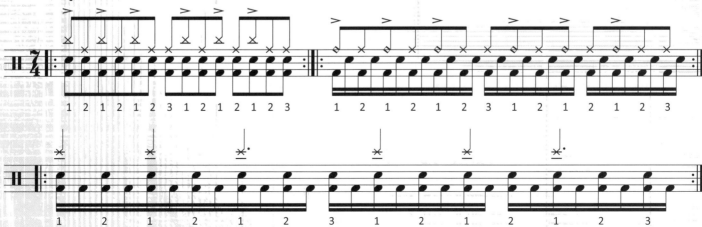

CHAPTER 8
ADVANCED DOUBLE-BASS CONCEPTS

You may have noticed that you had to deal with double-bass drumming in every chapter of the book so far. So why have another chapter on this? First, certain fields of double-bass playing have become more and more important for extreme metal drumming and, therefore, need to be reviewed separately. Second, it's my responsibility as a teacher to show you the more sophisticated concepts of double-bass drumming as well, even if they might be too advanced for some. I certainly do not know every reader personally and can't judge each one's individual level of playing, but over the years of teaching I found out that the concepts presented in this chapter have been highly appreciated by those students who successfully worked through exercises similar to chapters 1 to 5. Eventually this book should provide information and suitable exercises for players of all levels. If you are one of the more advanced players, you will have fun with the exercises coming up next, knowing that most other educational material is written for beginners and intermediate players. But also, if you do not consider yourself an advanced player, you can work out these exercises very slowly and return to this chapter every once in a while. So you'll have something to work on and to look forward to in the long run.

using polyrhythmic double-bass patterns

The following polyrhythmic approach to double-bass drumming is used more and more frequently by modern extreme metal bands. The most popular example is Meshuggah from Sweden, a band who likely gave birth to a whole new subgenre, the so called "djent," in which polyrhythms are used as the main stylistic element.

In example 8-1a you'll find a basic 3-over-4 polyrhythm. The hands keep a 4/4 half-time groove, while the bass drum is played on every third sixteenth note. If you understand this grouping as one sixteenth-note bass drum stroke followed by two sixteenth rests, you get groups of three layered underneath the straight backbeat played by the hands. Thus, you play three with the foot against four with the hands. It takes three measures to get back to the start.

TRACK 69

Example 8-1a

This basic bass drum phrasing can now be extended by subdividing the three sixteenth-note space into a group of two thirty-second notes and one sixteenth note, followed by a sixteenth rest.

 TRACK 70

Example 8-1b

In the same way you've built groups of three, you can also build groups of five by playing four sixteenth notes with the kicks followed by one sixteenth rest. So the pattern repeats after five sixteenth notes, which means you're layering 5 over 4 now.

 TRACK 71

Example 8-2a

Now you can insert some thirty-second notes, similar to example 8-1b. It will take five bars to repeat the whole phrase, which is an odd number to use for actual songwriting. Instead of playing the full five-bar circle, many bands tend to use an even number of measures and get back to the beginning after two or four bars, just skipping the fifth bar. This is done in example 8-2b, which ends after four bars.

 TRACK 72

Example 8-2b

In a similar way, you can layer 7 over 4. In example 8-3 you'll find groups of six sixteenth notes on the kicks followed by a sixteenth rest, while your hands keep the steady 4/4 pulse.

 TRACK 73

Example 8-3

You can add thirty-second notes to the 7-over-4 phrasing. In example 8-4, the seven sixteenth notes on the kicks are split into four thirty-second notes, four sixteenth notes, and one sixteenth rest. But don't worry about the math, just play the next example very slowly and add bar after bar.

 TRACK 74

Example 8-4

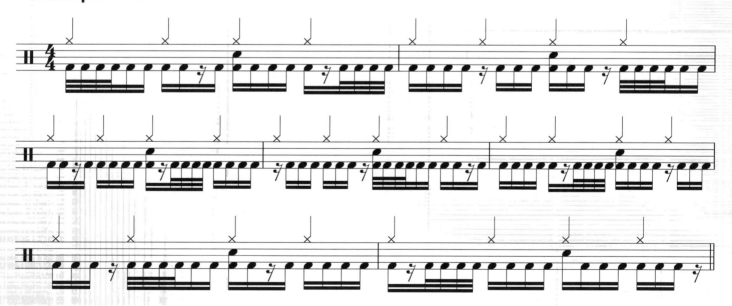

Manipulating Double-Bass patterns by using Polyrhythmic subdivisions

Time is relative. Funny enough, this saying by Albert Einstein also applies to rhythmic phrasing. The following exercises show more or less complex methods to manipulate a 4/4 time signature by playing shifting snare accents while keeping the double-bass pattern straight.

The first step to apply polyrhythms like that is to layer 3 over 4 by playing a steady 4/4 rhythm with sixteenth notes on the kicks, and then shifting the accents to every third note. By accenting every third sixteenth note, you create a triplet feel, even though you're still playing a straight binary rhythm. In example 8-5a, only the hi-hat accents shift to every third note while keeping the 2 and 4 on the snare. This adaptation will help you to get familiar with counting the 3 over 4 before shifting other groove components.

 TRACK 75

Example 8-5a

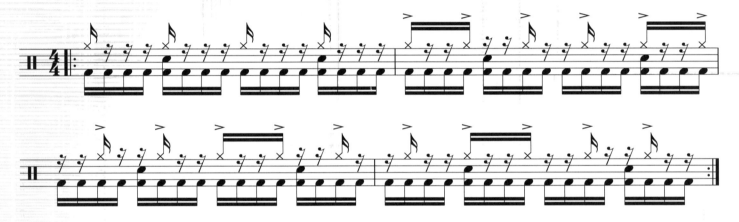

In a second step, the accents of the snare shift as well (see example 8-5b). To the ear of a listener who is inexperienced with these types of polyrhythms, the snare is the main accent of the groove. Thus, it is also the key to manipulating patterns. You'll hear this effect best when getting back to the straight 4/4 pattern. One huge difference is that the tempo seems to change suddenly. You get the impression that by accenting every third note, the tempo increases, but in fact, it remains the same. Getting the impression that the tempo got faster when accenting every third note is quite logical, because the space in between every accent gets smaller compared to the basic 4/4 groove in which you accent every fourth sixteenth note. So by knowing this principle, you can change the pace of a song and make it sound faster without actually changing the tempo itself. For keeping the time precise, you just always need to know exactly where the quarter notes are, even when you do not accent them.

TRACK 76

Example 8-5b

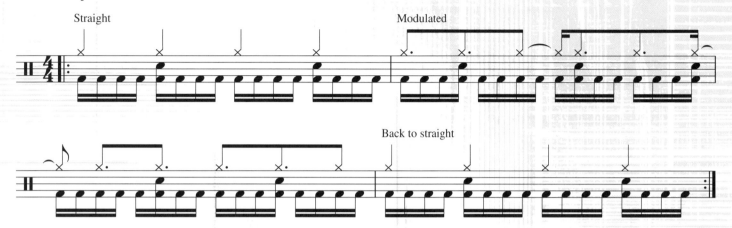

You can also move into a half-time triplet feel. The next phrasing would be more confusing, but it sounds heavier and even more unexpected.

TRACK 77

Example 8-5c

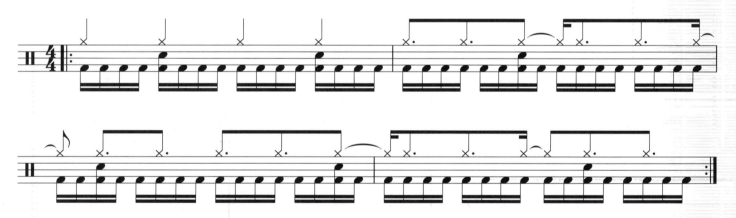

This principle of playing 3 over 4, and thus changing the time and tempo feel, sounds even more interesting when integrating rests. Example 8-6 works with a rest after every third sixteenth note and thus creates groups of three repetitive sixteenth notes on the kick drum. Then snare and hi-hat are shifted in the same ways as in examples 8-5, first in a half-time feel, then shifting into an upbeat feel.

TRACK 78

Example 8-6

The same method we used for layering 3 over 4 can now be applied to 5-over-4 polyrhythms. In example 8-7 the hi-hat first accents every fifth note, coming out of a straight 4/4 beat (variation A). It takes five measures to complete the whole circle and get back to the start.

A more common and accessible way of phrasing groups of five is to subdivide them into groups of three and two, counting **1**-2-**1**-2-3 while every "1" is accented (also see in chapter 7, "Odd Time Blasts"). You can find this phrasing regarding variation B.

The last, and very difficult, step is to apply the "triplet" feel by eventually changing the snare drum. In the last two measures of example 8-7, the accents shift back to straight quarter notes again (variation C).

TRACK 79

Example 8-7

Not surprisingly, the method can also be applied to 7 over 4. Example 8-8 subdivides the sixteenth notes in groups of 2-2-3 (which equals seven sixteenth notes) by accenting the hi-hat **1**-2-**1**-2-**1**-2-3. These hi-hat accents are now layered over the straight 4/4 snare beat. Getting back to the beginning of the phrase now takes seven measures.

 **TRACK 80**

Example 8-8

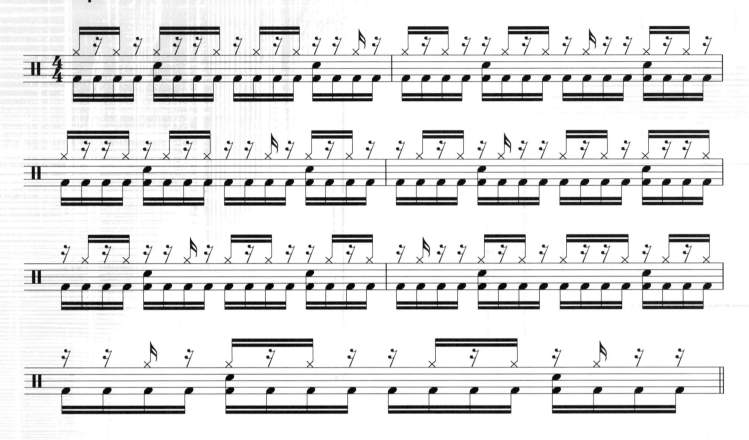

In example 8-8, the snare accents every third note, which creates the triplet feel we are used to by now.

There are many more ways to incorporate polyrhythms into a straight 4/4 groove and make the time feel faster by shifting the accents to every third note. Of course, you can also do the exact opposite and accent every fourth note of a triplet grouping. Example 8-9 delivers a straight 4/4 beat with the kick drums playing sixteenth-note triplets. The hi-hat begins playing on every eighth-note subdivision, playing eight strokes in total. In the second measure, it accents every fourth sixteenth-note triplet instead and results in only six notes. This creates a slower and more massive groove feel.

 TRACK 81

Example 8-9

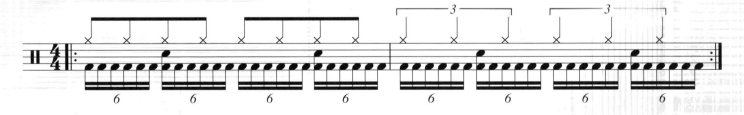

You can, of course, invert example 8-9 and go from a heavier pattern into the more forward-driven character of the straight 4/4 triplets. This way is likely used when releasing tension in a song structure.

quintuplets

In the same way you use triplets (playing three notes of equal length within a certain note value—for instance, within one quarter note), it is also possible to squeeze five strokes of equal length into one specific note value. Thus you get quintuplets (example 8-10), which create an odd-time feel even when you're playing a 4/4 groove.

 TRACK 82

Example 8-10: Quintuplets

The following exercises deal with this rather "under-explored" field of double-bass drumming, which certainly is about to play a prominent role in future extreme metal songwriting. Just like in chapter 2, "Breakdown Patterns," you can add groups of three, five, and eight, vary the hand pattern, or do both. Actually, at first I wasn't sure whether to include these exercises here. Eventually I decided that these exercises belong in the book because I used quintuplets in actual extreme metal songs of the bands I played in. In general, quintuplets do not appear as often as other concepts presented in the book. Maybe in a couple of years, working with quintuplets will be basic double-bass drumming knowledge, but it's not very popular yet. So by playing basic quintuplet patterns in a song, you have already moved into a field of applying double-bass technique that is not "the norm." Feel free to spread the word!

Quintuplet Exercises

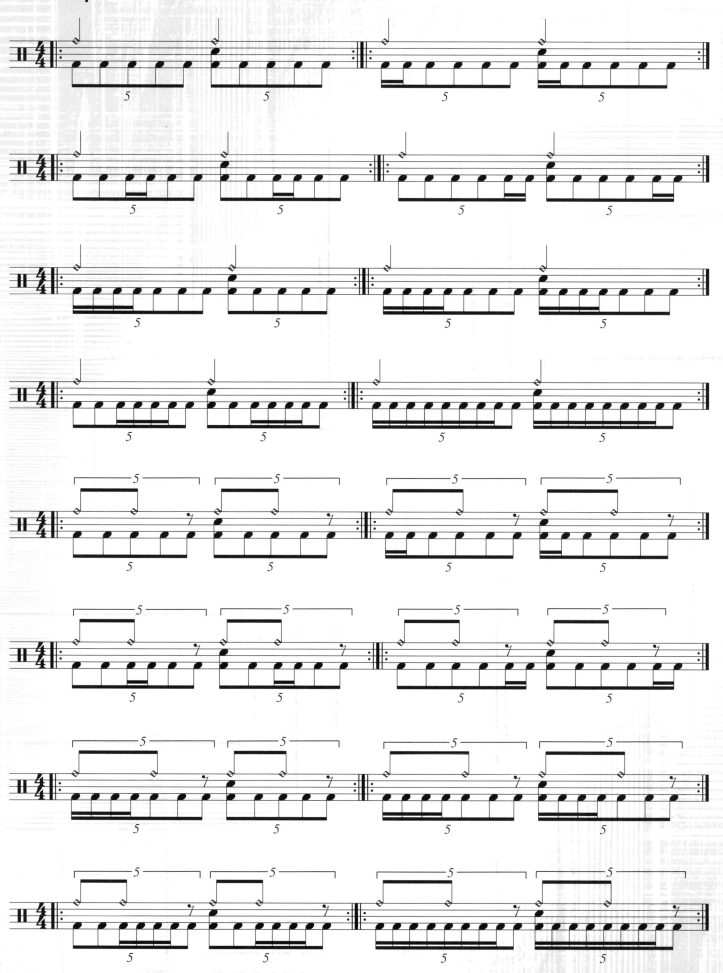

CHAPTER 9
EVADING HI-SPEED FOOT PATTERNS

So far this book has shown many different ways of practicing in order to get faster feet. When playing in an extreme metal band, sometimes there will be situations in which you will reach your personal limit but have to deal with it, somehow. Typically there are two situations I've experienced:

1. You have to play a foot pattern—for instance, a fast sixteenth bass drum roll—which is still a little too fast for you, and you'd need more time to rehearse to be able to fully control the pattern. However, there's a concert soon and you don't have enough time to reach the desired tempo.

2. You're not able to reach the speed you had a week ago and can't find the reason for it. Practicing makes it worse. However, there's a gig coming soon...

Since, in the long run, pushing speed limits takes a lot of time, you'll have to be patient and work on it, but that doesn't help you in these specific situations in which you have to play something and deal with your temporary limitation. In most cases, there are ways to elude your technical limitations in a musical way, which practically means to "downgrade" the tempo and, at the same time, keep the feel of the original drum line. The following examples show how to maintain a fast tempo by using fewer notes than originally intended, but keeping the song's drive.

In example 9-1, the desired pattern is a straight, ongoing double-bass downbeat at a very fast tempo, played for eight bars. At a quick tempo, the bass drum is the one component that means trouble. Sometimes, the musical intention stays the same if you turn an ongoing downbeat double-bass pattern into the evaded pattern of example 9-1, and thus turn long-term speed into short-term speed, which is easier to reach. A very important sound source in this example is the snare drum. It is the main groove component as it always accents the straight quarter-note pulse. The hi-hat is played on every even eighth note. By not changing the hands, both the original and the evaded patterns sound similar. So when downsizing the speed of the kick drums, the evaded pattern likely has the same musical intention as the desired pattern and thus resembles it effectively.

Example 9-1

The general method to evade fast double-bass patterns is to play fewer strokes with feet while hands stay the same. This principle can be used for upbeat patterns as well, which are just skank beats with ongoing double-bass sixteenth notes. If you can't play the straight double-bass sixteenths, just play two of the four sixteenth notes like in example 9-2, and there you go!

Example 9-2

When you play a backbeat variation and feel that the sixteenth notes with the feet are too fast, try switching to eighth-note triplets and see if they have the same musical effect as the sixteenths (see example 9-3).

Example 9-3

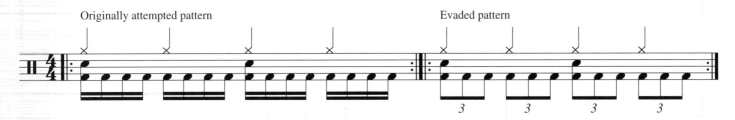

Sometimes triplets can be very fast. If you play example 9-4 at 140 bpm or beyond, you'll reach your technical limit very quickly. It is also possible to evade the fast triplet pattern by integrating a rest. Because every snare on a downbeat sounds like an accent, compared to the bass drums, the listener will first recognize the snare. So it becomes easier to the ear to "accept" the evaded pattern and not have the feeling that something is terribly missing. Sometimes a solution like this sounds even more interesting, because you do not just play many notes of equal length; instead, you create a more diverse pattern.

Example 9-4

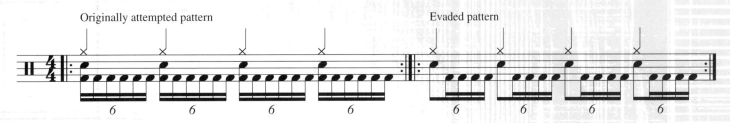

Of course, every evaded pattern is just a temporary solution, as each one has a slightly different feel than the originally attempted pattern. But when you find yourself being caught in one of the two situations described above, you'll appreciate the methods shown here. Always remember: There are solutions to any musical problem; it is not a sport, not a competition! It is absolutely okay to play slower if it suits a musical purpose.

Note: Situation 2
I've had many students who just couldn't pull off their initial top speed, even though they were able to play it once. I always told them to stop drumming for a week and just relax. After a week the tempo came back automatically. This happened in all cases! So I just assume that situation 2 is a result of overplaying. The only solution is to take a break for a couple of days to give the muscles time to recover. But be careful; you can really drive some people mad by compensating for the absence from playing with nervous tapping on tables, glasses, or knees!

Blast Beat support

There is no real way to evade blast beats. If they appear in a song, you'll have to somehow play them as expected. But if you have trouble with endurance and have to keep blasting through a longer part, you can insert some musical breaks, which do the song flow no harm. Example 9-6 shows a good way to place such rests and breaks. Sometimes these rests can even sound more appealing than a blast that never stops.

Example 9-5

CHAPTER 10 SONG EXAMPLES

After having learned and worked through the most common concepts of extreme metal drumming in chapters 1–9, you should be ready to play complete songs. I've written the three following songs to give you an idea of how the concepts can be applied in practice. All songs feature techniques and compositional tools covered in the previous chapters.

Song Example 1

This first song is fast and straight with a lot of influences from thrash metal music. The blast beat is used in the main chorus riff of the song, so play it with conviction and power.

Performance Notes

Section A	The song starts with the main riff as an intro. The drums accompany the riff along with the bass by playing various fills. The interspersed rests create suspense when leading into the blast.
Section B	This is the main riff of the song and could be interpreted as its chorus. The drums play an accented blast beat. If this is too fast for you, just play a skank beat here.
Section C	The verse of this song features an uptempo skank beat including several fast double-kick runs, which spice up the part.
Section D	This section features a lot of choked cymbals appearing in a non-alternated blast beat. Work through this part slowly and make sure to play it clean, since the bass guitar is playing along to the choked cymbal hits.
Section E	This part of the song is a typical double-bass downbeat, phrased as triplets. After three repetitions, the kicks change to fast sixteenth notes. If this is too fast for you, just keep the triplets instead.
Section F	The coda is the song's middle section, in which the drums play heavy tom grooves, as shown in chapter 6.
Section G	The main riff is interpreted as a ride-cymbal groove variation, similar to the ones learned in chapter 6. Make sure to play each stroke loudly in order to sound heavy!

Structure: A – B – C – D – E – B – D – F – G – C – E – B

TRACK 88 · 89 (PLAY-ALONG)

song Example 2

This song features mostly triplet blasts and grooves, similar to the ones used in brutal death metal. This will teach you a practical example of using triplets effectively.

Performance Notes

Section A	The drums start with clenched cymbals and then move into a heavy triplet tom groove without using the snare. Step-by-step, the drums increase the amount of notes played and thus the musical tension.
Section B	The drums play a triplet bomb blast here (see example 3-2b) with the left hand playing the quarter-note accents on the China cymbal.
Section C	Here the drums execute a reversed skank beat first, then change into a regular one. Now the rhythmical code is no longer in triplets; be careful not to rush when shifting to a binary rhythm.
Section D	Shifting back to triplets we find a heavy tom rhythm played in a half-time feel. Actually, with the guitar riff being slow, you could play anything that fits the quarter-note subdivisions. So if you want to come up with a drum line yourself, feel free to improvise.
Section E	After section B is repeated, the drums move into a regular triplet blast. This part resembles the riff of example 7-9. After the traditional triplet blast, the drums change to bomb blasts and thus maximize the musical intensity. You can also shift the accents on the China cymbal for more variety, as in examples 7-10.
Section F	In this part, the tempo changes from 130 to 115 bpm. Also, the drums slow down and play less. After this section you go back to section C. Be careful as the tempo changes back to 130 bpm.
Section G	The ending section of the song exactly features the drum line of the doom part in example 6-18, with the tempo changing to 70 bpm. Try to maintain a laid-back feel here, even when moving into the faster double-kick pattern.

Structure: A – B – C – D – B – E – F – C – D – B – G

TRACK 90 · 91 (PLAY-ALONG)

song example 3

This more melodic song is an example of enduring blast beats played for a large number of measures. Even with the blast being "only" at 192 bpm, the song will help you improve your long-term speed and endurance.

Performance Notes

Section A	Similar to song 2, this song starts with an intro in which the note value becomes faster and faster. You don't need to stick to this notation exactly, it is just important to get the idea behind the increasing note values, which again is to increase musical tension.
Section B	The drums play a sixteenth-note double-kick rhythm in 12/8. Sometimes there are hand patterns in unison with fast kick drums, with the right hand playing on the ride and the left hand playing on the hi-hat or also on the ride. If you have problems playing these patterns, go back to chapter 2 and synchronize your hands with your feet.
Section C	This part always starts with a 4/4 drum fill leading into a 6/4 traditional blast beat. This blast should be interpreted as "legato-blast" (see examples 7-6).
Section D	This section is something like a verse featuring ongoing traditional blasts. Make sure to maintain the legato feel of section C. After this part you'll have to repeat sections B and C, so save some energy for later.
Section E	The coda in this song builds a long middle section. After having played a variation of part C, the tempo drops to 96 bpm, which is half as fast as the rest of the song! The riff progression you learned in example 6-14 is used here.
Section F	In the solo of this song you'll find a 3-over-4 polyrhythm. For an in-depth explanation, check out example 8-1b. After this part the tempo changes back to 192 bpm and part C is repeated.

Structure: A – B – C – D – B – C – E – F – C

TRACK 92 · 93 (PLAY-ALONG)

A Intro

♩ = 192

B

C

Play 4x
On D.S. play 2x

To Coda

D Play 4x

D.S. al Coda

Coda

E Play 4x

CONCLUSION

Congratulations! It must have been a long and exhausting journey to finally reach this page. After having worked through all the exercises in the book, you should now be able to master a big part of today's standard extreme metal drumming, and even more. After all, the biggest reward for the hard work is to sit behind the kit and enjoy the skills you've been building up in the last months. But now it is not the time to lay back and relax, thinking that these new skills will endure. Unfortunately, they can go away without further practice, especially when speed and endurance are concerned. The best way for you to reestablish your drum knowledge in a musical way is to find other musicians to play with. Writing your own songs and creating something unique is probably the hardest thing in music. And I hope this book was able to help you build the foundation for expressing yourself musically with other people who constantly encourage you to practice and improve. At least, I hope you had fun exploring this book. I surely had fun writing it.

ABOUT THE AUTHOR

Hannes Grossmann is the drummer and one of the main songwriters of the German extreme metal band Obscura, with whom he recorded and released the critically acclaimed albums *Cosmogenesis* and *Omnivium*. With the bands Obscura and Necrophagist (for whom he recorded the album *Epitaph*, which marked a milestone in the extreme metal genre), Hannes extensively toured throughout the world. He is also a member of instrumental metal band Blotted Science, with whom he recently released the album *The Animation of Entomology*.

Being an active member of the German drumming community, Hannes plays many clinics, drum festivals, and educational performances for his endorsers. He also released the double DVD *Progressive Concepts for the Modern Metal Drummer* and teaches students from all over the world through his website, **www.hannesgrossmann.com**.

YOU CAN'T BEAT OUR DRUM BOOKS!

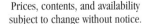